Italian – Yes!

Italian – Yes!

Italian-American Women's Club

To order additional copies of this book, contact:
Xlibris Corporation
1-888-795-4274
www.Xlibris.com
Orders@Xlibris.com
121614

Contents

Italian—Yes!

The title of our book says it all. We are a group that formed a club to express our joy and pride at being Italian. Our culture is so rich since Italy was invaded by Greeks, French, Spanish and Normans and each enriched the Italian culture by leaving a bit of their own.

Italians have customs that date far back in history. The St. Joseph's Table is one of them. A table is laden with delicious food and many are invited to partake of the ethnic foods.

At Easter Time, Italians make Pane Cena, bagel-like bread with a cross cut into the dough. The taste of anise is a reminder of the importance of Easter in their lives.

On the feast of Epiphany, Italians celebrate little Christmas, the day La Befana, the Christmas witch comes to reward good children with gifts. Bad children receive a piece of coal. Hopefully there are not too many that are "bad".

Italians have a great sense of humor; they find things to enjoy when there is not much to laugh at. They also have a great spirit of compassion, especially for the poor or oppressed.

In Italy, when the Jews were hunted down and killed, Italians risked their lives to save them. They hid them for months, taught them to speak Italian and then passed them as relatives. Compassion was the factor that saved many lives.

Sister Mary Ventura O.P.

I was born Mary Ventura in Bradley, Illinois. I am now the Co-founder of the Italian American Women's Club with Annette Dixon. This book is our story.

My father, Philip Ventura, was 16 years old when he decided to leave his beloved Sicily and travel to America. He had several good reasons to do so, since his father died and he felt responsible to help earn money so his family could survive. Also, he knew, there was little hope of helping his family if he remained in the small town of Caccamo, a farm village with few opportunities to earn money.

Dad's family consisted of his mother Giuseppa Mendola, his sister Marietta and two brothers, one of whom, Santo, followed him to America and became a barber in Chicago. Giovanni, his adopted brother, was killed when he was quite young. Very little is known except, that he was missed by his grieving family. Dad never shared too much about his death.

Dad made the long and arduous trip to America on the Conte de Savoie, a ship with few conveniences for poor people who paid a minimum fee. However, he never complained and soon joined the hundreds of Italians who settled in the Chicago Heights area and found a factory job. The pay was meager by our standards but enough to allow my father to send money to his family in Italy and save some to ensure the future he envisioned. This included marriage and property he could call his own.

Philip married Josephine Ciaccio in the beautiful St. Rocco Church in Chicago Heights. They moved to Bradley in Illinois and purchased a two-story home that cost all of $5,000 dollars. This was to be their home for many years to come. In fact, family members still live there.

My early memories are filled with happy family events. Josephine was born first, then I came along and was named Mary after my father's sister Marietta. Frances was the third girl to arrive and was named after my mother's sister Frances Patti. We always got along and were great companions for each other.

In the days before TV and video games we enjoyed simple pleasures. Rainy days were our favorite because we could go outside and splash in the puddles and cool off in the rain. When we tired of this we went into the house, dried off, and put on clean clothes. We then played monopoly for hours until we were called to a meal or had to do chores.

From first grade on, school was a constant joy for me. I looked forward to the mile walk and to the new things I would learn each day. Every teacher was dedicated and great.

Learning to read was the best thing that ever happened. I loved it so much I would go to the library and take out several books. While I was reading them, I was transported from the present to wonderful adventures that left me breathless. I often got into trouble when my father would call me and I was so immersed in what I was reading, I couldn't hear him.

By the time I was in fourth grade I had read every book in the children's section of the library. The librarian said I could begin reading the books in the adult section. What a thrill that was! I devoured books about other countries and travel. It was almost as good as actually going there. In real life the farthest I traveled was from Bradley, Illinois to Chicago, a sixty-minute trip.

While in my teens, all that changed. I had been going to the public school in Bradley from grade One to second year high. Now I was on my way to Springfield, Illinois to follow my vocation as a Springfield Dominican. I entered on Labor Day and enrolled in Sacred Heart Academy the next day. I completed my Junior and Senior year and graduated at the end of the year.

My next educational adventure was to attend Springfield Junior College with the Ursuline Sisters as my teachers. They were great educators and I remember them fondly.

My education continued at St. Joseph College in Rensselaer, Indiana. Saint Joe is a coeducational, private Catholic liberal arts college and my major was English with a minor in Spanish.

From there I went to the University of Illinois in Champaign and completed my Masters in Administration and Supervision. This allowed me to direct a migrant program for the Federal government in Mendota, Illinois and to qualify me to be a Principal in Aurora and Morrisonville, Illinois. However, I decided my true love was teaching so, I once again began working directly with students.

In 1996 our principal, Sr. Ann Brummel decided we should do something for our students who were struggling. She did some research and found a company (CEI) Creative Education Institute, that had a program that seemed promising.

ELS is a program that helps students become independent learners. It not only teaches students how to read, it also helps them to comprehend more easily. It accelerated learning by teaching students how to focus, concentrate, process, apply and become academically successful.

My youngest students are four years old and my adult students 40, 58, 59 and my oldest was 80 years old. I do enjoy working with the different age groups. It is so satisfying to see their progress and the smiles on their faces as they achieve success. No other pay is necessary. I always say I work for God and He pays later. That's good enough for me.

My Italian culture and background have been a big help to me as a teacher. I bring to the classroom my deep love for family, an Italian trait. This helps me to accept each child, no matter what faults or lack of knowledge. My philosophy is, "God doesn't make junk" so every child can learn. It is my job to find the way that works for each child. I expect the most from each student and they rise to the occasion and do their best. If a child fails to learn I take it as a personal failure. That is why very few of my students have failing grades.

Another trait that I learned from my Italian family is to challenge my students to do the best they can do. My father was great at giving me the confidence I needed to do even more than I thought I could. In education this translates to success for students who are willing to try. They find they are more capable than they thought.

Italians are positive thinkers and find ways to bring joy to their lives in spite of everyday ups and downs. In the classroom this translates into students who realize today may be tough, but tomorrow is a new beginning. Since they may not even remember the problems they had yesterday, why fret today. Worry only makes problems seem worse than they are.

My Sicilian father had a special saying I found very helpful. He always said, "You don't have to be a carpenter to build something." What he meant was that with a lot of thought and a bit of imagination, you could figure out how to do almost anything.

With this in mind we were able to build a chicken coop, tar the roof to prevent leaks and repair almost anything. For the difficult repairs we hired an expert and stayed with him the entire time he was working. The next time the repair was necessary, my father and I were able to do the job and so saved lots of money.

A funny thing happened when I was about twelve years old. My father took the time to teach me how to paint and I became very good at it and loved to paint next to my father. He painted the high parts of the room and I painted the lower sections.

One day I said, " Dad, you are dripping paint on me." He smiled, got off the ladder and said, "Want to try it?" I was thrilled, climbed up and began painting. From that day on, whenever there was a room to paint, I did it from the top to the bottom. Dad would only watch me, a proud look on his face.

Perhaps the most important thing I learned from my father was how to handle pain. Since his father died when he was seven years old, he had to support his family. As a hired hand at that tender age, he was expected to be ready to do the farmer's bidding at any time of the day or night. Wearing his shoes so he would be ready caused many foot problems later in life.

As a grocer who was on his feet twelve hours a day, he was in constant pain. You would never know it to see him at work. When I asked him about it, he reminded me, if it is something you can't do anything about, learn to live with it.

To be constantly fretting about pain will not help the pain go away. It will only feel worse.

Since all of us have pain at one time or another, I found his advise to be invaluable. In the morning when the alarm rings, I hop out of bed fast. I never ask myself how I feel. Once I am on my feet, it is too late to moan and groan and fall back asleep. So, I get ready for the day. This has allowed me never to miss a day of school, due to illness for over fifty years. Ignoring small pains has become a habit.

I mentioned my father was a grocer and our store was a family affair. We were all proficient in lending a hand, stocking shelves, taking care of customers, making change and anything else that needed to be done.

One day when I was the only person taking care of the store, five men came across the street from the railroad tracks. Two stayed outside the store, three entered and walked around. I went into alert mode, since I sensed something was not right. Sure enough, one of the men came around the counter toward the cash register. Imaging his surprise when he saw me with a gun pointed toward his middle, safety off and my finger on the trigger. You have never seen men take off so fast in your life!

At that moment my father entered the store and shouted "Mary, don't shoot!" He grabbed the gun and chased the men down the street.

When he returned he told me never to kill a person over money. When I asked him why he kept a gun in the cigar box next to the cash register, he said it was only to scare people. He taught me the value of life and that it was too precious to end it on my own. Only God had the right to do that.

When dad died at the age of fifty-nine, my sisters insisted the gun had to go. Since they were too afraid even to pick it up, I took it to the back yard, dug a deep hole and buried it. I guess it is still there.

You have read so much about my father, you are probably wondering about my mother. When Uncle Joe was in the U.S. Army he visited his home in Sicily. On his return he brought his sister Josephine Ciaccio to America. There she met Philip Ventura and they were married at St. Rocco Church in Chicago Heights. Later they moved to Bradley, Illinois purchased a house and began their family. Santo was born first and died when quite young. Josephine followed, then I came along and lastly Frances.

I can remember my mom scrubbing the kitchen, cooking the delicious meals and sewing all our beautiful clothes. She was an expert seamstress and she kept us looking great without spending much money on clothes.

Since my mom died at the age of forty-three and I was only seven, my memories of her are limited. However, I do remember vividly being in school and one of the students very hurtfully saying, "You don't even have a mom." When I started crying Miss Dressler, one of the teachers, talking with me and trying to console me.

The Dominican Sisters taught CCD classes and told us to make visits to the church. I was so devastated I decided to go to the church since it was only about 2 1/2 blocks from school. I knelt before the statue of Mary. Her arms were outstretched and she looked down at me. I said, "I don't have a mother." In my heart I heard her answer," I will be your Mother." That message consoled me beyond words. I left the church, but my heart was filled with peace.

One incident that happened right after my mother died is a permanent part of my memories. Aunt Frances, my mom's sister came over and ripped out the hems of each of the dresses my mom had sewn for us. She carefully made them much longer. As soon as she left, my dad who had never used a sewing machine in his life ripped out the new hems and sewed them back the way my mom had made them.

I learned a lot from the way my father handled the situation. He didn't argue with my aunt, but he allowed her to do what she thought best. Then he proceeded to honor my mother's wishes. What a kind and gentle man!

As soon as you hear the word Italian, the next thought that comes to mind is food. Food the necessity that is so very available to those close to the land. There is never a need to worry about healthy eating since vegetables and fruits are easily grown in the homeland. Healthy eating becomes a habit and is carried over to life in America.

At our house we always planted several acres of garden. First we turned over the soil using a garden fork. Then we planted tomatoes, corn, beans, asparagus, celery, swiss chard, zucchini, Italian squash, green peppers, lettuce and fennel. We also planted radishes, carrots and many other vegetables. We were the proud owners of a variety of fruit in our backyard. Our grapevines provided grapes and our trees peaches, pears, cherries, plums and figs. There is nothing better than fresh fruit that is picked ripe and eaten. The taste is so different from store bought produce. We enjoyed it very much.

Since we grew the zucchini, squash and peppers in our own garden and made the Italian Sausage at home, our meals were inexpensive but delicious. We also canned dozens of jars of tomato sauce made with our vine-ripened tomatoes. You can't beat the fresh-made taste of sauce that has simmered for hours.

I would be remiss if I didn't go on with my life story. When I was about nine years old, my father decided to go to Italy and get married. He said it takes a woman to raise girls and he was probably right. So off he went to Caccamo, Sicily and married Caterina Dioguardi, a friend of his family and a very talented seamstress. She made wedding clothes and even men's suits. Actually, there wasn't much she couldn't do.

Dad stayed in Italy the better part of a year and Aunt Rose, Uncle Leo and family moved in with us. We missed Dad, of course, but grew to love our cousins Josephine, Anthony and Marie. We played with Marie and treated her like a doll. She was so tiny and somewhat frail so we played a trick on her. Everyday when I milked my goat we would put the rich creamy milk in a regular milk bottle and put it in the store. Whenever Marie wanted milk we poured her a glass of the goat's milk. It was so nourishing she soon became very strong. As a teen she became a tennis champion and later joined a religious order, CND of Canada.

I remember the day our new mom arrived from Italy. We went to Chicago to meet her and I got to sit on mom's lap. However, since I was somewhat frightened, I sat stiff as a ramrod. Dad must have noticed because when we got home he reminded me to show her only love and respect since he would not tolerate any other actions.

Life changed for us with Caterina in the house. She loved to cook so we had many delicious meals. Her sewing talent provided us with new clothes and her Rizzo relatives a whole new group of people to love.

Aunt Jo and her small son Joey spent many summers with us. Since Aunt Jo had arthritis, mom decided good meals would help her get well. She had some form of chicken for all three meals fried, roasted, boiled or made into soup. Can't say it cured her but everyone was happy trying. We loved having her with us because she was always cheerful and happy. Aunt Jo had a somewhat unique voice and even now I can hear it in my head and it makes me smile.

Italians think of food as an excuse to socialize. Everyday it was a chance for everyone in the family to get together, eat and talk. On Sundays it was a special meal consisting of spaghetti, meatballs and homemade sausage in a delicious red sauce we called sugo. The sauce had to simmer a couple of hours and the house was filled with a delicious aroma.

After mass we were allowed to take a slice of freshly baked bread and put some sugo in a bowl and dip the bread in the sauce. It was a treat that we looked forward to and is a precious memory that our modern day Prego brings to mind. However, Prego and even Francesco Renaldi sauce never come near the special taste of slowly simmered sauce. Perhaps the oregano, garlic, basil and other seasonings made the difference.

Meat was not eaten everyday but vegetables were fixed in a variety of ways and tasted so good we didn't even miss the meat. However, I remember that even during the depression my father grilled porterhouse steaks for us once a week. He wanted us to be healthy and strong and we were. I never remember going to the doctor for any reason until I was a teenager.

One day I told my father I felt sick. I was probably ten years old. Dad took me into our store and gave me a chocolate cup cake. In five minutes I had eaten it and was in my way outside to play hopscotch. Dad must have guessed I was a bit hungry and tired. The food was what I needed for a quick recovery.

I want to share with you some of my favorite recipes. They are simple but make for a quick and easy meal.

Zucchini Casserole

2 medium Zucchini or 4 small, sliced
2 cans diced tomatoes
Chopped onion to taste
Chopped green pepper to taste
1 jar prepared tomato sauce
1-cup mozzarella cheese, shredded
1/4-cup Parmesan cheese, grated

Place zucchini is a microwave safe container and microwave until partially cooked, not soft.

Microwave peppers and onions until soft

Place zucchini, diced tomatoes, onion, green pepper, tomato sauce and mozzarella cheese in oven safe casserole. Sprinkle with Parmesan cheese.

Bake at 350 degrees for 50 minutes or until cooked and bubbly hot.

Italian Squash

1 Italian Squash
Olive oil
Parmesan Cheese
Cut squash in 1/4 inch slices.

Fry in hot oil until soft and light brown on both sides.
Drain and place on paper towels.
Sprinkle with Parmesan cheese.
Serve hot.

Easy Crust Pizza

1 lb. ground beef
1 lb. Italian Sausage
1 8 oz. jar tomato sauce
1 tsp Italian Seasoning

Brown beef and sausage; drain and add sauce and seasonings. Set aside.

1 cup flour   1 tsp salt
2 large eggs   1 tsp oregano
1/3 cup milk   Grated Parmesan cheese

In a bowl combine flour, eggs, milk and seasonings. Mix well. Pour batter into a pan and cover the bottom completely. Carefully place drained beef and sausage mixture over the batter. Sprinkle with Parmesan cheese.

Bake at 425 degrees about 40 minutes or until bubbly and well cooked.

BBQ Country Ribs

1 pkg. Country Style Ribs (6)
1 jar BBQ Sauce
Honey
Heavy Aluminum Foil

Line a tray or pan with aluminum foil with at least four inches of foil above the edge of the pan. Place ribs in a single layer not touching. Drizzle ribs with honey. Cover ribs generously with BBQ sauce. Use additional foil to form a tightly sealed cover. Do not let foil touch the tops of ribs.

Bake at 425 degrees for 1 1/2 to 2 hours or until tender

Stuffed Green Peppers

6 med. green peppers	1 egg
1 lb. lean ground beef	1/4 tsp. onion powder
1/2 c. bread crumbs	1/2 tsp. Italian Seasonings
1/2 c. Minute rice	Salt and pepper
2 c. Tomato Sauce	1/4 c. Parmesan cheese

Wash peppers, cup off tops and remove seeds. Microwave until beginning to get soft. Set aside to cool.

In a bowl combine beef, breadcrumbs, rice and egg. Add seasonings and cheese and mix well. Stuff the peppers with the mixture. Place peppers in a deep pan. Pour tomato sauce over the peppers and allow to drip over. Bake in a 350-degree oven for about 75 minutes.

Parent's Wedding

DAD, JO, FRAN AND I

Grade 8

Postulant

Novice and Sr Margaret
Sienna

Nature Lover

BEST FRIENDS

SISTER MARY VENTURA OP

CELEBRATING LEONARDO DA VINCI AWARD

Young
Professed

CATERINA DIOGUARDI VENTURA

50TH YEAR CELEBRATION

Virginia Anne Naso Morgan

I was born on July 23, 1936 and named Virginia Anne Naso. (They tagged me Ginger, however, from day one and I love it!) Since I was an only child, you can imagine the joy of my parents and the special place I occupied in their lives. They were there for me and I always knew I could count on them for anything I needed, even beyond what the typical Italian family traditionally provided. I always knew I was loved and grew up with that feeling of self-confidence.

My grandparents on my mother's side were Antonio Coglianese and Maria D'Amato. They were born in Oliveto Citra, Italy (Salerno) and arrived in America on December 26, 1906.

Money was scarce for the young couple so Antonio's father-in-law paid for their trip, a good example of how important family is to Italians.

My mother's siblings were names Maccario (Michael), Loret (Loretta), Vincenzo (James), Rosina (Rose), Carmi (Carmen), and Eny (Anna), my mother.

My father's mother Diega (Della) Serio who was 18 years old, wanted to come to America to marry her sweetheart Agostino Naso who had already come to Chicago. Diega's father would not allow her to arrive in Chicago unless she was married, so, she was married to Agostino by Proxy, then sailed to America. Agostino who had been previously married and widowed was already the father of twelve children. His first wife Rose Dangelo had died and still being a fairly young man, he was ready to re-marry.

After Diega and Agostino set up home in Chicago, my grandmother had thirteen pregnancies of which only five children lived. Count them—my grandfather was the father of twenty-five. The five who survived were Ignacio (Nat), Josephine, Maria, John and Antonino, (Tony) my father.

I never knew my grandfather as he passed on years before I was born, but, "Nanna" was with us until she turned 84 years old, living independently in her own apartment until she passed on. She was delighted when our first daughter was born and she could see her Great Granddaughter.

"Nino" as my father was called as a young child by his family was born and raised in Chicago's Chinatown. He was so proud of that fact that every year during Chinese New Year Dad would take us back to the "Old Neighborhood" to renew old memories and to meet some of his "Old Friends" still living in the area. Nino was a three-year-old child when he fell and fractured his hip so severely that he spent the next three years in a full body cast as an inpatient at Children's Memorial Hospital of Chicago. During this time my father missed much of his family life including the death of his father Agostino Naso. As he grew up, "Tony" was not able to keep up with many of the activities that most of his friends were involved in because he was left with one leg shorter than the other, which resulted in a limp for most of his life. Because of his restrictions he learned to play the guitar and became the center of most parties and gatherings for the remainder of his life. Daddy had me at his side everywhere we went, playing his guitar and teaching me to sing all the songs of the times, everything from his favorite "Just a shanty in Ole shanty town" to "You are my sunshine."

Daddy also taught me just enough Italian to be "Cute", but not enough to understand when he and my mother wanted to converse without me knowing what they were talking about. I could understand him when he would call me) Venire Qui) come here, or Chiuso La Paorta, close the door, Mangiare, eat, or Faccia Brutta, ugly face, and best of all, Bella Figlia, beautiful daughter. He would then ask me Capisce", understand, and I would say "di" Papa! He would tenderly kiss me and say "Buona Sera", How Italian, How beautiful! By the way, my father's parents were born in the town of Termini Imerse, Palermo Italy.

"Annie", as her family called her, grew up in that cottage that her father built. She had a pet goat that she would feed and milk daily, her mother used the milk to make cheese for the family recipes.

She lost her father when she was only 8 years old and became very close to her mother Maria who was a very serious diabetic. Anne's older siblings worked outside the family home, but Anne grew up helping her mother keeping the house, cooking and baking bread every morning. In 1932, when Anne was 16 years old and had graduated from Harper Jr. High School, her mother died in a diabetic stroke. Anne was left at home, keeping the family home for her five siblings. As each brother and sister married and left home, my mother met my father at the age of 17 years old and were married three months after she turned 18. Mom never worked a job outside of her home, but kept an immaculate house, was an incredible cook and took care of my dad until the day he passed at age 71. They raised me, their only child with the love and passion that I would not be a "spoiled brat." She did amazingly well on all counts and lived until she was 92 years old, driving her Portofino Blue Ford until she was almost 90 years old.

As an only child, I led a charmed life, (not spoiled but charmed). I attended Hedges Elementary School in Chicago from grade one through grade five. I took tap dancing lessons and music lessons, participated in recitals and assembly shows and was always part of the volunteering groups. I then transferred to Edward Elementary School for grades six through eight and graduated among many of my closest friends with whom I am still close. While I was in the sixth grade I was confirmed and took my Sponsors name of Giovanna. I still love that name and love my sponsor Giovanna as well as her husband Nicholas, who, by the way was my Godfather when I was baptized. My mother's sister Rosina was my Godmother. I loved her too. I went to Thomas Kelly High School in Chicago, had four very active years there and I graduated in June of 1954.

While in high school I met my future husband Donald Lee Morgan. He was the youngest of seven children and became the joy of my life. Since we planned to get married, my parents decided I should not go to college. This was the usual way of thinking in the 1950's. Don and I married on October 20, 1956 and rented an apartment in Chicago for one year. Don enlisted in the Armed Forces and was called into service on our First Wedding Anniversary. Since I was about to find that I was pregnant with our first child, I moved back to my parent's home. Donald completed his basic training in Colorado and then spent the next two years of active duty in Germany and returned to Chicago in 1959 to meet our fifteen-month-old daughter Donna Lee.

You can imagine how happy my parents were to have me living with them while my husband served his country. Their joy was even greater when their first grandchild was born in

1958. They were able to enjoy and observe the first year of her life. It was a time of peace and happiness for all of us.

When Donald returned to Chicago we rented an apartment and continued our married life. Our second daughter, Mary Christine was born on Christmas day in 1961. Our family was now growing and we led a happy life.

In 1970 we decided to move to Oak Lawn, leaving the familiar area where we were born and where much of my family still resided. My grandfather Antonio built a cottage shortly after he arrived in America. Not only was I born there, as were my children, but many of our family members. My mother and six siblings and several of my cousins were also born there.

Speaking of cousins, being an only child, my cousins were as close to me as siblings would be. We spent so much time together I was never really lonely—holidays, summer vacation time, always relatives nearby. Those of us still surviving are still very close as are our children. "THAT'S ITALIAN"

When Donald and I moved to Oak Lawn, IL we purchased a house. This was our first home and the home that we still live in now.

Beginning with graduation from high school, I have had a very busy and interesting business and social life. After my senior year in high school, I became a secretary at Continental Casualty Company in downtown Chicago. I later pursued my other jobs as a Loan Secretary and Closing Coordinator in the Real Estate and Mortgage Banking business. The last thirty-five years I have spent in the Funeral Industry as an Administrative Assistant.

I was President of B.P.W., Business and Professional Women for two years and a Red Hatter for ten years. I also spent ten happy years as a Girl Scout Leader working with Brownies through Senior Scouts and even taking them away to camp.

My job today is still in the funeral industry. Since my retirement seven years ago, I have been a community representative promoting the business through the Chamber of Commerce in Oak Lawn as well as the Evergreen Park Chamber of Commerce where I serve as Secretary and Treasurer. I have been appointed a Senior Commissioner in Oak Lawn for the past 8 years and hope to continue working with the Senior Center on projects and ideas to keep the seniors always active and healthy in our community. Also, I have been president and now treasurer of our Italian American Women's Club.

Perhaps the most enjoyable part of my social life was as a singer and dancer and stage performer for St. Gerald's Showtime. What a great opportunity to meet many people and bring them wonderful entertainment.

My husband Donald's life was enhanced for twenty-five years as a football coach in the Catholic School League to elementary students fourth through eighth grades. Fall was always his most enjoyable and exciting time of the year!

Thinking back, I realize the Rev. Michael Hack has been an important factor in my life and the lives of our family. He has been instrumental in celebrating our children's weddings, the baptisms of our grandchildren, the important anniversaries in Don's and my life, the most important our Golden Anniversary in 2006, and even the Funeral Masses of my parents. He is our dear friend.

Don and I are now enjoying our four grandchildren. Our daughter Donna and her husband David's son Anthony Michael Alvarez is now a sophomore at Florida State University in Tallahassee, Florida and is pursuing a career in Law. He will spend his spring semester in London, England studying toward that goal.

Our daughter Mary's eldest son Donald is in his third semester of college. His interests are more toward technology. Mary's middle son Mark is in his senior year of high school, more interested in photography and Emily Elizabeth Taylor our youngest and only granddaughter is a freshman in high school. Her interests include her position as a "flyer" on the Jr. Varsity Cheerleading squad and whatever studies she can fit into her busy life after that. Great "Kids" and we're proud of each of them.

My wonderful parents are not with us any longer. "Papa" who always called me his "Bella figlia" and played his guitar while teaching me to sing along with him passed away in 1984 and Mama who always reminded me that she came second on

Papa's life (after I was born), lived until she was 92 years old, independently until she was 90 years. She was the greatest ethnic cook ever—her "Pasta fagiol" was unmatched. She taught me so much. I miss them both.

One of my special pastimes is to think back on my life and to realize how very lucky my family and I have been. In spite of life's ups and downs, we have always been aware of how God has given us the grace to overcome adversity and go on with life, trusting in His loving care. God has blessed us and we are very grateful.

As a very famous Italian Chef (and most of my non-Italian friends have often confessed), "There are two kinds of people, Italians and those who wish they were Italians".

I'm so proud of my Italian heritage!

Here are some of my favorite recipes:

Artichoke Salad

1 can drained and washed
Artichoke hearts
1 small green pepper, chopped
1 small onion, chopped
¼ lb. mushrooms, sliced
½ tsp. minced garlic

Salt and pepper to taste

1 tsp. oregano
¼ c. olive oil
2 T. cider vinegar
Green olives &
chopped celery (opt.)

Quarter artichokes, rinse well. Add all ingredients, mixing well. Cover and refrigerate (marinating) at least 24 hours.

Funghi Imbottite (Stuffed Mushrooms)

1 lb. lg. mushrooms	3 T. butter
3 T. grated Parmesan cheese	6 T. olive oil
1 T. chopped parsley	1 c. Italian breadcrumbs
1 clove garlic & sm. onion, minced	Dash of salt & pepper

Clean and remove stems from mushrooms. Mix breadcrumbs, cheese, salt, pepper, parsley and soft butter with fingers until mixed together well. Fill indentation in mushroom caps. Pour 2 tablespoons oil into bottom of baking pan. Place mushrooms, stuffed side up, drip remaining oil over mushrooms. Bake 20 minutes in medium oven until tops are brown. Serve hot.

Artichoke Spread

1 can artichokes, chopped   1 c. mozzarella cheese, grated
¾ c. mayonnaise   1 c. parmesan cheese, grated

Mix ingredients together and pour into baking dish. Bake at 350 until it bubbles. Serve with crackers or snack rye bread.

Mama's Pasta Fagioli

1 lg. (48 oz) jar Randalls Great Northern Beans
1 medium onion
Sm. pkg. ditalini pasta
Grated cheese, salt, pepper, and oregano

Sauté onion in olive oil until soft, empty beans (including liquid) into pan. Simmer 10 minutes. Cook pasta al dente, reserve 1 cup of water when draining pasta. Mix pasta into bean mixture seasoning with salt and pepper plus a pinch of oregano. Pour enough reserved water into mixture to make soupy. Simmer 10 to 12 minutes. Sprinkle with grated cheese and serve with crusty bread. Buon Appetito.

Hot Bagna Cauda

2 sticks butter   ¾ c. wine vinegar
3 heads garlic, minced   12 oz. flat anchovies
2 c. olive oil

Sauté garlic in butter over medium heat. (Don't scorch or burn.) Add anchovies and oil together, simmer for about ½ hour. Just before serving, add vinegar and simmer a few more minutes.

Variation: You may substitute ½ cup cream for vinegar.

Note: Bagna Cauda comes from the Piedmont area of Italy. This savory sauce is kept simmering in the center of the table while diners dip their raw vegetables and Italian bread into it.

Insalata Patate (Italian Potato Salad)

4 lbs. potatoes (cooked whole)   4 med. tomatoes
1 lg. onion   1 sm. green pepper
1 T. sugar   ¼ c. chopped parsley
Salt & pepper to taste   ¼ c. each: olive oil,
                                   wine vinegar

Slice cold potatoes, onion and tomatoes and add chopped green pepper and parsley. Toss, mixing well. Serves 6.

Tomato and Mozzarella Salad

6 lg. tomatoes, sliced   1 purple onion, sliced
8 oz. mozzarella cheese   12 whole fresh basil leaves

Dressing:

3 T. olive oil   ¼ tsp. oregano
3 T. red wine vinegar   Pepper to taste
1 garlic clove, minced   3 fresh basil leaves, coarsely
                                chopped

On a bed of lettuce, arrange tomatoes, cheese, onion and basil. Mix all ingredients together and pour on top. Garnish with sprigs of basil.

Mamma's Spinach and Potatoes in Broth

2 T. olive oil

4 med. potatoes, peeled, quartered and parboiled

2 garlic cloves, minced

2 lbs, spinach, well washed

1 c. chicken broth

1 c. water

Place oil in a large saucepan and gently brown garlic. To the pot add chicken broth, water and the potatoes. Add spinach. Cover and cook 15 minutes. This is a soupy mixture but the garlic, potatoes and spinach mingle. Serve with Italian bread.

Escarole and Beans

1 c. chicken broth

1 lg. head escarole (well washed

2 T. olive oil

2 garlic cloves, minced

1 (15-oz.) can cannelloni beans and coarsely cut)

4 fresh basil leaves cut up

In a large saucepan, place chicken broth and escarole, bring to boil and simmer for an hour. Gently brown the garlic in the oil, then add cannelloni beans with their liquid and heat thoroughly. Combine with escarole and let simmer for 10 to 20 minutes. Stir carefully with wooden spoon. This should have a soupy consistency (add a little more broth, if necessary). This is excellent with hot pepper flakes, grated cheese and hot Italian bread.

Zabaglione (Italian Pudding)

6 egg yolks
6 tsp. sugar
6 T. amaretto or Marsala wine

1 tsp. grated orange peel
½ c. whipping cream

Combine egg yolks and sugar in top of double boiler and beat with a wire whisk until frothy. Add amaretto or Marsala and grated orange peel. Place over gently boiling water and beat continuously until smooth. Remove from heat and place, still in boiler top, over ice cubes in bowl to cool. Then whip cream and fold into cool custard with a rubber spatula. Pour into individual serving cups and chill. Serve over poached pears or peaches, or as a layer in strawberry shortcake. Sprinkle with shaved chocolate, if desired.

Quick Tomato Sauce

2 T. olive oil
2 cloves garlic, minced
1 lg. can crushed tomatoes
Salt & pepper to taste

½ tsp. oregano
1 T. fresh basil, chopped
1 T. sugar

Simmer about 30 minutes. Pour over favorite pasta.

Papa's Lasagna

3 T. olive oil
Onion powder
Garlic powder
2 tsp. Italian seasonings
2 lbs. ground chuck
1-lb. can tomato puree
2 (6-oz.) cans tomato paste

1 c. water
1 T. sugar
1 T. fresh basil
Salt & pepper
4 c. shredded mozzarella
1 pkg. lasagna noodles

Brown ground beef in olive oil, cooking until beef is no longer pink. Add puree, paste water and sugar, seasoning to taste. Simmer 1 ½ hours stirring often. Meanwhile cook lasagna al dente according to package directions. Coat bottom of baking dish with ½ cup sauce, then begin layering lasagna alternating with meat sauce, cheese and noodles, ending with sauce and layer of shredded cheese to top. Bake at 350 for 35 to 40 minutes.

Note: you may also cook tiny meatballs in sauce and layer them between layers of lasagna.

Carne Pizzaiola

2 lbs. top sirloin steak

4 potatoes, sliced thick

2 onions, sliced

Lg. (26 oz.) can tomato sauce

½ tsp. oregano

Salt & pepper

Spray 6-quart casserole with nonstick spray. Spread bottom of casserole with tomato sauce. Begin layering with potatoes, meat, onions, sauce then seasonings, ending with potatoes and sauce on top. Bake at 350 for approximately 2 ½ hours.

Stuffed Shells Florentine

4 c. your favorite marinara sauce   1 egg
2 lbs. ricotta   1 pkg. jumbo shells
1 pkg. chopped frozen spinach   Grated cheese

Spoon 1-cup warm marinara sauce onto bottom of large roasting pan or large rectangle baking dish. Cook spinach as directed on package, drain well. Mix with ricotta cheese, egg and 1 tablespoon grated cheese. Cook shells according to package directions, drain. Fill each shell-using teaspoon with cheese mixture. Arrange shells in single layer on sauce in pan. Bake at 350 for 20 minutes. Serve with reserved hot marinara sauce.

CARMEN
7-19-15

VINCENZO (JAMES)
6-5-11

MARIA
(MOTHER)
5-20-1877

LORETTA
2-14-09

ENY (ANNE)
4-28-16

ANTONIO
(FATHER)
2-14-1875

ROSINA
(ROSE)
11-20-13

MACCARIO
(MICHAEL)
1-5-08

Picnic Grove along the road.

1940

Paulina Barraco

I'm now known as Mama Barraco but my name at birth was Paolina. My parents were hard-working and dedicated and were born in Marsala in Sicily. In order to find work and better their conditions, they crossed the Mediterranean Sea and settled in Tunisia in Africa.

My father was a carpenter and my mother a dressmaker. They were able to make a comfortable living and in 1934 welcomed me into the world. However, my stay in Tunisia was quite short since fear of W.W. II helped my parents decide to move back to Sicily.

My childhood was spent enjoying family and learning to cook, clean and sew by watching my mother and following her example. It never fails to amaze me how all I learned formed a basis for my future life.

At the age of fourteen I joined my mother in her business as a dressmaker/tailor. We sewed wedding dresses, men's suits, work clothes or anything our village people needed. Our most unusual request was for a mattress. We could and did fulfill any and all requests.

In 1952 at the age of eighteen, I married Vito Barraco. He was a hard working young man from a large family and so wanted a large family with many children of his own. Our first three children, Phyllis, Vincent, and Salvador were born in Marsala, Sicily.

By 1960, my husband once again found a way to better his family. By special arrangements he moved our family to the United States and settled in the Chicago area.

While Vito worked as a grocer, I stayed at home with our children. Nick and Francesca were born here and soon I had five children attending Catholic schools.

So many memories come to mind but one particular one changed my life. We were living in Harvey and had a large yard behind our house. I always washed the clothes and hung them on the line. My husband wore white shirts so I washed them and using a bit of bluing in the rinse water. This made them appear dazzling white.

In the neighborhood lived Sister Agatha and since she taught at the Catholic school my children attended she asked the children how their mother got the white clothes so clean. She said, "Ask your mom if she will wash the altar linens for me."

I agreed and in return, Sr. Agatha helped tutor my children and made sure they had their homework. It was a great exchange and lasted about five years. My children benefited greatly from Sister Agatha's influence and so did I.

Although we lived in many places, we always tried to hold on to our traditions. Sundays were always special and began with everyone dressing in their best clothes. Almost everything my children wore was homemade since I was a seamstress. Only a few dollars would buy enough material to outfit each child. They always looked great and fit in well with the other children.

Mass was at nine and we attended as a family. After mass we hurried home to make the sauce and always added sausage, meatballs, and chunks of beef. The delicious aroma that filled the house was memorable.

While the sauce simmered we decided on the dessert. A favorite was homemade cream puffs or biscotti. They were served with a wine and even the children were allowed to partake. It was a time for lively conversation and laughter.

Sunday afternoons were usually spent visiting relatives or occasionally going to a movie. It was a time to relax and spend quality time with family and friends. It was a day we looked forward to during our busy workdays. Sunday was special.

Holidays were always celebrated according to traditions and often involved special foods. On Christmas Eve, we served wedding soup and many kinds of fish followed by a dessert. Spingi were usually made and served hot. They were fried dough that reminded you of a powdered donut but were tastier.

On Christmas day we enjoyed cotoletie or breaded steak, salad, fruit, and coffee. Of course the meal was followed by the gift exchange and many cries of joy and surprise.

We looked forward to New Years Eve because tradition called for arancini or rice balls. At the center of each ball was a surprise treat of fresh peas and mozzarella cheese. Arancini were a family favorite.

Pasta a Forno was our New Years Day meal. It consisted of pasta, ground beef, peas, and sauce. It was simple to make but thoroughly enjoyed by all.

Pane Sqarato or boiled dough provided an excellent breakfast on Easter Day. The dough was embedded with hard-boiled eggs and served with hot chocolate. It was a meal we never failed to enjoy.

Our noon repast featured a roast and some kind of pasta. Lasagna was a good choice and of course it was always freshly made. The ricotta and other cheeses gave it a flavor not to be forgotten. Salad, vegetable, and dessert with wine rounded out the Easter meal.

For the children's birthdays we served the traditional panetoni, cake with candles. A special dinner chosen by the celebrant was also part of the day. Gifts were a must and friends often shared the celebration.

Armed with many authentic Italian recipes, Vito and I thought we would try our hand in the restaurant business. My husband would handle the pizza and I would do the cooking in the kitchen. Our first restaurant was on Kedzie and we had a successful five years there before we moved to a larger location in Evergreen Park. We have been there 30 years and continue to be successful.

Some of the other locations where we started restaurants were Crestwood, Burbank, Orland Park, Crest Hill, and Lisle. My son Vince manages Crestwood, and Fran, Sam, and Nick manage Evergreen Park. My grandchild Danielle manages the restaurant in Orland Park on Wolf Road. Dominic is in charge of the carryout on 159th in Orland.

As you can see, all the restaurants are family managed. That makes it mandatory to make sure the food we serve is the best it can be. We do that by using family recipes and all fresh ingredients. Our cheeses are authentic and purchased from firms that make them fresh. No time or effort is too much as long as the finished product fulfills our standard for excellence.

When I make meatballs, I use 75 pounds of meat. One part is pork and two parts beef. It never ceases to amaze me that my recipe brings delight to the lives of so many.

I've been in America for fifty years and I love this country that has fulfilled my greatest dreams. However, there is a special love in my heart for my Italian roots. I will always love Italy and visit it as often as I can. I am Italian-American and proud of my heritage.

Here are some of my favorite recipes:

Anisetta Biscotti

2 cups flour	4 eggs beaten
1 cup sugar	1 stick butter
2 Tbsps. Anisetta	1 Tbsps. Baking powder

Place ingredients in large bowl and blend for 7 minutes.

Bake in 2 loaf pans for 20 minutes at 350 degrees. Cool for 10 minutes. Remove from pan and cut into half inch slices. Place slices on sheet pan and cook for 6-7 minutes more.

Oraangini

1-pound regular rice. Cook for 20 minutes with 2 chicken bouillon cubes. Boil with 5-6 cups of water. Strain until dry. Cool for 1 hour. Then add 3 large eggs or 4 medium eggs, 1 cup Romano cheese. Add ¼ cup cooked sauce to make rice a pink color.

Recipe for sauce for ground beef: Heat 2 tablespoons olive oil to cook small onion. Add ½ pound ground beef. Cook together and add 8 ounces of tomato sauce and cook for ½ hour.

Phyllis Louise Naso Pinotti

My name is Phyllis Louise Naso Pinotti and even though I was born during the Great Depression (1932) I lived a simple, modest life. I am known affectionately as, "the girl of The Depression" by my granddaughter, Gianna, since like her American Girl doll "Kit", I was born during that period of time.

My grandparents, Agostino and Lodavica (Geraci) Naso were born in Termini Immerses in Sicily and immigrated to the Chicago area in the late 1800's. My grandpa worked as a peddler with his own horse and wagon. My grandparent's raised ten children in a small house on 22nd place in Chicago now know as Chinatown.

My parents, Philip Joseph Naso and Jeanette Stolfe were also raised in this neighborhood. They were married on June 15, 1930 and I was born on February 28, 1932, which was in a leap year, which meant that everyone born on February 29th had a birthday every four years.

My maternal grandparents were Carmen and Della (Iacullo) Stolfe born in New Jersey and Regiliano, Italy. They had six children until my grandmother died during the influenza epidemic of 1917-1918 at the age of thirty-seven.

Since my father had a job as a salesman in a large food store in downtown Chicago, we always had enough food to eat. A simple method of credit began during The Depression years. The grocer would carefully write down all of our purchases in a black book and at the end of the week, when Dad got his paycheck, the grocery bill would be paid.

We heated our apartment with a coal stove and my father chopped wood and carried it up to the second floor. Sometimes he would let me help him. Eventually, we got a gas heater. We kept our food cold in an "icebox" where we put a sign in our window to order the size block of ice we wanted . . . usually a 25 or 50 pound piece. When the ice melted, the water dripped into a pan on the bottom of the icebox. It was my job to empty the pan of water every day.

I also remember a telephone box on the wall where we would drop "nickel" coins to make a phone call. We were given coins called "slugs" a few per month to also make phone calls. Once a month the telephone man came to collect the money from the coin box.

There were many enjoyable times with my parents. My father took me to Chicago White Sox baseball games and my mom took me to the ball game on "Ladies Day" when the tickets were 25 cents each. We also went to the World's Fair downtown by the lakefront in 1933. I do remember holding onto my father's hand so tight because I was afraid I was going to get lost. Shopping with my mom and helping with the cooking and baking were very pleasant memories. I also remember going downtown once a month to have lunch with my mom and aunts at the Woolworth's Dime Store. My favorite meal was roast beef with mashed potatoes and gravy over a slice of bread with a chocolate soda.

When I was 12 years old, my brother Philip Charles "Chuck" was born in 1944, and we moved to a larger apartment. I had fun taking care of my baby brother, as I was 12 years old.

Holidays were always fun because all my aunts, uncles, and cousins would come to our house since my mother was the oldest in the family. She was known as "Momma Jeanette" by her younger brother Charlie.

When my mother made her homemade ravioli it was my job to press the edges with a fork to keep the square edges from opening up. I would then put them on a clean white cloth to dry before cooking. Today, I still cook a homemade pot of spaghetti sauce with meatballs and sausage for my family. Desert consisted of homemade "S" cookies, "Thumbprints", nut cups, and pound cake.

A polio epidemic in the 1930's so frightened my mother that she decided not to send me to kindergarten. I went to public grammar school and started first grade at the age of seven. While going to school during World War II, I was in charge of collecting, weighing, and with the help of the boys, tying bundles of paper, which were donated to the war effort. During that time I made my First Holy Communion and Confirmation, in a program, which would now be called "C.C.D." I graduated from James Ward School in 1945.

When I entered Visitation High School in 1945, there were very few Italian students as we were outnumbered by Irish, Polish, German and some Croatian girls. One Monday I brought a leftover meatball sandwich for lunch. A girl at our table commented that my sandwich smelled good and asked if I would like to trade half of my sandwich with her. When I found out her sandwich was bologna, I politely said, "no thank you." Sunday's leftover meatballs made a great Monday school lunch.

Getting to school was a challenge, since the "street car" was the only mode of transportation. No one was dropped off at the door or got picked up after school. Your travel schedule had to match the streetcar schedule; many times I had to run to catch the streetcar. I graduated from Visitation High School in June of 1949.

I attended evening classes at DePaul University's Business School twice a week. I took business classes and worked for an insurance company as a secretary to pay for my classes.

I spent many hours at the beach and roller-skating with my best friends, Gloria and Rosalie. We also liked to dance and did so twice a week. At the age of 18 in 1959, I was in a wedding party with a neighborhood young man who was to become my future husband, Art Pinotti. Being in the wedding party was the beginning of a beautiful friendship and we were married on September 6, 1952 at Santa Maria Incornata Catholic Church. For our honeymoon, we drove to Daytona Beach, Florida in a car loaned to us by Carmen, my husband Art's brother. We enjoyed watching car races, dog races, and beautiful beaches.

After returning to Bridgeport, we both returned to our jobs. I worked for an insurance company and my husband worked as an automotive parts salesman. We lived in a modest four-room apartment where I met my lifelong best friend, Mary. In 1953, I was pregnant with twins. We were very excited because Art had a twin sister who died at an early age and my father had twin brothers, one of whom died at the age of three. However, it was not meant to be since I suffered a miscarriage after two months.

In 1956, we were blessed with a son, Gerald Philip, a healthy baby boy. In 1957, a baby girl was born. Unfortunately, since the baby was born prematurely, she only lived for a day. We named her Roslyn.

Imaging our joy when in 1960, during a fierce snowstorm, Janet Marie our tiny daughter was born. Five years later in 1965, James Philip "Jimmy" was born. Each birth was the occasion for great celebration since family is very important in the Italian cultures as with many cultures. We then moved to Evergreen Park, Illinois in August of 1965.

In August of 1967, our whole family was involved in a very very serious auto accident in lake Geneva, Wisconsin. We all sustained many injuries; the most serious were my husband, two year old son, Jim and myself. I sustained many broken bones, which took two years of doctors, surgeries, and therapy to recover. Mostly today I suffer from major arthritis problems but my children and husband recovered nicely. Thank God our families, neighbors, friends, sent food and many prayers to help us. We thank God that we all lived after such a serious accident.

Back to business . . . in 1956, Art and I opened a small auto parts store in Bridgeport called Parnell Auto Parts. He would stock shelves and go for parts that customers ordered via phone. While running a successful business for many years, Art and I raised three children, Jerry, Janet, and Jim and put all three through college. We participated in three weddings and were blessed with four grandchildren.

My children all married. Gerald married Cheryl Alebich and has two daughters, Alexandra Michele and Maryl Louisa Pinotti. Janet Marie married Michael Kuehn and has one son Zachary Michael Kuehn. James married Camille Jandacek and has one daughter, Gianna Maria Pinotti.

Also close to my family is my brother Philip Charles Naso, who is married to Therese Hedinger with one niece Christina Marie Naso who married Steve Bonnell.

As the years went by, my husband Art retired and then became ill and lost his battle with kidney failure and died January 1, 2000, the year of the Millennium. We miss him dearly.

With my grandchildren growing up, I have watched them with great love. Alexandra graduated from Concordia University and is pursuing a Master's Degree in Social Work at the UIC Jane Addams College of Social Work. Her sister Maryl is currently attending Concordia University and playing NCAA volleyball as her sister Alex did. My two younger grandchildren are currently attending Junior High School. Gianna at Central Junior High and Zachary at Plum Grove Junior High.

Over the years with the passing of parents, I took over some family traditions such as Christmas Eve Dinner with ravioli, meatballs, and homemade cookies. The grandchildren would often exchange presents after dinner and have fun.

I still enjoy attending the feast of St. Joseph's Day on March 19th and the Santa Maria Incornata procession, which honors the birthday of the Blessed Mother on September 8th.

With my family members married and living their daily lives, I am now free to do volunteer work. During the past school years, I have offered my services to St. Bernadette School where my children and grandchildren attended school, helping in the library.

I now focus my attention to Little Company of Mary Hospital in Evergreen Park. I volunteer in the Pastoral Care Department answering the phone, doing clerical work, and any other necessary tasks needed to ne completed.

I belong to the Italian American Women's Club and am very happy to be with ladies of my culture where we enjoy each other's company, recipes, and traditions. I am really grateful for them.

Here are some of my favorite recipes:

Cup Cake Cookies (Nut Cups)

1 stick Imperial or Butter   1 3oz. pkg. cream cheese
1 cup flour

Filling:

¾ cup brown sugar   1 dash of salt
1 beaten egg   1 tablespoon butter, melted
Few drops of vanilla   1 cup chopped walnuts

Bake at 375 for 12-20 minutes. Sprinkle with powdered sugar. Do not grease tin. Place each cookie on tiny cup tins.

Swiss Cheese Chicken

4 Chicken Breasts   1 pkg. Swiss cheese
(8 pieces deboned)

Place pieces of swiss cheese on top of chicken in Pyrex Dish. Cover chicken with one can cream of chicken soup, ½ cup vermouth (dry white wine). Sprinkle 2 cups Pepperidge Farms Herb Stuffing over chicken. Melt one stick of Imperial and drizzle over chicken. Cook covered 1 hour at 350. Uncover and cook an additional ½ hour.

No Bake Rice Pudding

2 cups uncooked rice (no minute rice)

Cover with water, one-teaspoon salt, one cinnamon stick, and lemon rind (size of half dollar). Bring to a boil until rice is absorbed by the water. Add one gallon of milk a little at a time. Let boil for about half hour. Remove lemon and cinnamon stick. Add one-teaspoon vanilla, four scoops of sugar. Come to a boil again. Let cool and refrigerate.

Mary Lou Apicella Gorka

How lucky can you get? In 1938 I was born into a loving Italian family and named after my grandmother, Mary Louise. On my mother's side, our ancestors came from Bari, Italy. My father was born on Chicago, but his parents were from Naples.

My father was a hard worker and got his work ethic from his father. On his first job at Dearborn Glass Company, he met his wife to be, Catherine. They married and had for children, Alfonso, Concetta, Thomas, and me.

My mother was a typical Italian housekeeper and wonderful cook. When we knew were going to have company for dinner, we all went into action. Someone picked the ripe beautiful tomatoes from the garden for the delicious sauce. The unforgettable aroma as it simmered was a background for the two hundred ravioli my mother would make.

My mother always allowed us children to help. It helped us to bond and appreciate our close Italian ties. We always felt great happiness to be working together.

For dessert we always had pies, either fruit or crème. Since her crusts were made with Crisco, the results were fantastic. We could never get tired of her pies and remember them fondly to this day.

My mother was an excellent seamstress and could sew just about anything. She could also crochet and make me a beautiful crochet dress that I dearly loved. Her other creations included crochet tablecloths, doilies, comforters, edged pillows, hankies, slippers, and many more useful things.

My family lived upstairs in a two flat. Since my grandparents lived downstairs, I spent a lot of time with them. In the evenings, I would go downstairs and listen to the radio. Then my grandmother and I would have hot tea, crackers, and jelly.

My mother's family lived on the north side and once a week, we would all get together for a wonderful dinner. It was a time of family closeness and typical conversations we all enjoyed and looked forward to. It was also an opportunity to do many fun things with my cousin Lu.

An interesting fact about my father comes to mind. On his birth certificate his name was Dominic but it was not spelled correctly. His friends all called him Dom and then it turned into Tom. Later he legally changed his name to Thomas.

I began my schooling at the age of five in kindergarten at the Mark Sheridan School at 28th and Wallace in Chicago and continued there until I graduated from eight grade. I loved school and was always a good student. In fourth grade I was double promoted and my teacher, Mrs. Wolfe and I kept in touch for about 10 years.

I attended Kelly High School and in my last year I got a part time secretarial job at the Federal Reserve Bank downtown. When I graduated in 1955 I got a full time job and worked there for several years.

I loved to walk down Michigan Avenue and shop or sit on a park bench and eat my lunch while I enjoyed the sun. Working at Santa Fe Railroad on Michigan and Jackson made this easy.

I have always been religious, following the example of my parents. I attended All Saints Church on 25th and Wallace Street. I was involved in their Teen Club run by a young priest, Father Ciezadlo. He did a great job of making the club very successful.

The Teen Club gave me an opportunity to do a lot of volunteer work. We also went on picnics and had dances. My friend Beverly and I taught the younger boys just entering the club to dance. The club also provided entertainment since we had pool tables, a jukebox, and ping pong tables.

Every Sunday, I sang in the choir and made many good and caring friends. I dearly loved All Saints Church and all its precious memories. It was with great sorrow that in 1958, the church and our home were knocked down to provide the I-55 expressway.

I met my husband Stan and went out with him for 2 ½ years and then married him. We lived in the McKinley Park area so when my parents had to move, they moved close to our apartment. We really enjoyed having them so close.

We had our first child, David Alan in 1959. Of course we were overjoyed and especially since he was a healthy and lovely baby.

Our second child, a beautiful girl, was born in 1960. We named her Kathleen Mary and were so grateful to God for our good fortune.

We had our third child, Mark Joseph in 1961. We were so happy to have this beautiful and healthy baby boy. We were grateful to God for all his blessings.

As my children got older, I was able to get several jobs. I was a waitress for a while and then had a full time job as a secretary to the Plant Managers at a chemical company.

When my children were teens, I wanted to be home with them when they came home from school so I got a part time job at Dominick's. I was a bagger for three months, and then moved to cashier. I loved the contact with people and found this to be very fulfilling.

After three years, I moved on to a job in Accounts Payable and worked there for fifteen years. I also went to Real Estate

School and loved helping people sell their homes or find their dream homes.

My next job was at Queen of Peace High School. There I met many loving, caring, and supportive people. I am still friends with many of them and enjoy all the years I worked with them.

After seven years, I retired and so did my husband. Since then, we have enjoyed our leisure time.

Our children have gone on to have beautiful careers. Dave and Mark worked in the Corporate Computer World for 20 years. Then they decided to open their own computer business. This is very successful and I am grateful to god.

Dave and Mark also have a musical career. Mark is the music coordinator at St. Stevens Catholic Church. Both boys play the guitar and sing at the masses every Sunday. They are also involved in Community Theater and have a "Praise Band" which performs at church and in concerts.

Our daughter Kathy has a wonderful career in the field of education. What could be better than to teach our future generation? Kathy teaches math to eight graders at a middle school. She excels at what she does and enjoys working with her students very much. Teaching is a career that is very fulfilling and reaps benefits that reach far into the future.

Stan and I are so very proud to be grandparents of nine children, eight girls and one boy. We are also proud of the success of our own children. God had truly blessed us.

Our first son, Dave, married a wonderful girl. Diane. It was so exciting planning our first wedding and such a relief when it turned out so well. Dave and Diane had three children, Nicole, Brian, and Lauren.

When our daughter Kathy married John, we were very excited. Planning a daughter's wedding is a bit different but great when it becomes a beautiful memory. John and Kathy were blessed with three girls, Katelyn, Michelle, and Kristina.

When our second son Mark married Jennifer, we were more relaxed in our planning. Everything went well and we enjoyed the wedding. They were also blessed with three beautiful children, Rebecca, Jessica, and Victoria.

All of our grandchildren are very successful. One is in the computer business with his father and uncle. Another graduated with a degree in Economics and plans to have her own beauty salon and spa. Two are in the education field and are teachers.

We are also proud of the younger grandchildren as they continue their education and decide on their futures. We know they will also be successful and we thank God.

Our grandson Brian was a very fine soccer player when he was in high school. His team was able to go to Europe and play in Italy, Germany, and Switzerland. What a wonderful opportunity to travel and get to know people from those countries. The trip was made possible by volunteer parents who earned the money to pay for the trip for the soccer team.

1970 was the year with a surprise business venture. Stan and I along with two partners decided to purchase a restaurant. We learned by trial and error how to manage the place, make a profit and provide delicious meals. We learned as we went along and my sister and I even became bartenders when necessary. However, when we lost our lease that was the end of our business. We learned a lot and had no regrets.

Now I want to tell you about my husband Stan. He is of Polish and German decent and grandpa wanted to know why I didn't go out with an Italian boy. Of course, he was teasing and when the family got to know him they were more than pleased.

Education was very important to Stan. He attended St. Maurice Grammar School, De LaSalle High School, and received a two-year degree from Wilson Junior College. He stopped going to school to work and save for our wedding. We got married and had three children, and then he went back to school.

After ten years of going to school part time, at the age of 32, he had earned a degree on Structural Engineering. He always loved his job and excelled in his career. We are so proud of him!

We are now enjoying our retirement. We spend our winters in our condo in Florida. We have many friends and enjoy their company immensely. We call them our second family.

Stan retired at the age of 65 and enjoys fishing, golfing, and playing tennis. He also enjoys playing his harmonica and listening to music. After a very rewarding life it is great to relax and enjoy life.

Family is so important to the Italian Culture. I am so happy to have been born Italian and to have enjoyed all it has meant to me.

Traditions are important. When I was very young, I remember our family always having a vegetable garden. This was a very important tradition and for my parents it was also economically good. We had many different kinds of plants such as tomatoes, peppers, cucumbers, eggplants, and many other different kinds of plants, not to mention a variety of spices, most importantly, basil and parsley which were used very often to make wonderful spaghetti sauce for the spaghetti dinner we had every Monday.

So I grew up with this wonderful tradition and it followed me throughout my life for which I am very grateful. Each year my mother and father planted and took care of our wonderful garden. Every summer, we had many varieties of vegetables in the house left on our counter to ripen before cooking and processing them in jars to be used throughout the winter. We would even help by picking weeds and removing the vegetables, which were ready to be brought into our house.

My parents concentrated primarily on our tomato plants because of their importance in making our most beloved spaghetti sauce, which was so important for preparing our spaghetti dinners, which was our specialty when we had company over for dinner. Then one day, our tomatoes were discovered big time. A reporter from the Chicago Sun-Times newspaper heard about our very healthy tomato plants, which at this point my mom and dad had upgraded their tomato crop to the point that the tomatoes were one to two pounds in weight and were about the size of a grapefruit. They made the newspaper! The reporter came to our house to interview my mom and dad and to look at our tomato plants. My mom even got her picture in the newspaper. So many people that saw this article in the newspaper called to congratulate my mom and dad on their success in growing the biggest tomatoes in town. We were proud!

We loved this tradition and learned a lot about growing tomatoes and other plants and when I got married, my husband and I started a vegetable garden and to this day, we are making our spaghetti sauce. Our children are grown and married and have tomato and vegetable plants and life goes on.

I am truly grateful to my parents for passing on this wonderful tradition which was passed on to them by our grandparents and which their ancestors passed on to them. TRADITIONS IN OUR ITALIAN HERITAGE ARE IMPORTANT!

Here are some of my favorite recipes:

Cannoli Cake

1 pkg. (18-1/4 oz.) white cake mix

Cannoli Filling:

2 pkg. (8 oz. each) creamed cheese, softened
1 carton (15 oz.) ricotta cheese

1 cup confectioner's sugar

1 tsp. vanilla extract

½ tsp. almond extract

1 jar (16 oz.)
Maraschino cherries
1 cup miniature
chocolatechips

Frosting:

1 cup shortening
1 cup butter, softened
1 pkg. (2 lbs.) confectioner's sugar

1 cool whip

3 tsp. vanilla extract
4 to 5 tbsp. water
Pink and green gel
food coloring

Prepare and bake cake according to package directions, using two greased and floured 9-inch round baking pans. Cool for 10 minutes before removing cakes from pans to wire racks to cool completely.

In a large mixing bowl, beat cream cheese and ricotta until combined. Add confectioner's sugar and extracts. Drain cherries well, reserve 1 tsp. cherry juice. Chop cherries. Stir chopped cherries, chocolate chips and reserved cherry juice into ricotta mixture. Refrigerate for 1 hour or until spreadable.

To assemble, split each cake in half horizontally. Place one layer on a serving plate; spread with a third of the filling. Repeat layers twice. Top with remaining cake layer. Frost cake top and sides with cool whip.

Ricotta Soup

½ lb. very thin egg noodles
1 lb. ricotta cheese
½ cup oil
1/8 cup Romano or Parmesan cheese

1 tsp. salt
¾ tsp. pepper
1 egg
1/8 cup parsley

Boil noodles in medium size pan until slightly done. Pour out some of the water. Water should cover noodles slightly. Mash ricotta cheese with fork in dish. Then add the oil, Romano cheese, salt, pepper, and parsley. Let this come to a boil. Then turn to simmer. Add ricotta cheese and egg. Break egg yolk with fork and swish around in soup. Let soup cook until egg is not soft (about 5 minutes). Taste soup. If it needs more seasonings, add to soup right away.

Italian Spinach Soup

1 pkg. frozen leaf spinach	2 small cloves garlic, chopped small
1 small potato	1 tsp. salt
1 can Great Northern white beans	¼ tsp. pepper
1/3 cup oil	

Cook spinach according to instructions on box. Cut potato into small pieces and cook in separate pot of water until done. In pot or frying pan, sauté garlic in oil. In strainer, rinse and strain beans. Then add water to pot of spinach (about ½ to 1 inch above spinach). Then add garlic, potatoes, beans, and salt and pepper. Bring to a boil, then simmer and cook for 5 to 10 minutes until garlic has flavored the liquid. Add more seasonings if needed.

Italian Meatballs (Great Grandma Apicella)

1 lb. hamburger	1 egg
¼ c. bread crumbs	1 Tbsp. parsley
1/8 of an onion, chopped	2 cloves garlic, chopped
½ tsp. salt	¼ tsp. pepper
1 Tbsp. Parmesan Cheese	

Form meatballs and either drop in spaghetti sauce before sauce is done cooking or bake in oven on 325 for 25 to 30 minutes and dip in sauce later.

Spaghetti Sauce (Great Grandma Apicella)

(This is a double recipe for another meal)

2 cloves garlic, chopped
2 tsp. parsley
¼ tsp. pepper
2 lg. cans (32 oz.) plum tomatoes

¼ onion, chopped
1 tsp. salt
2 tsp. basil
6 cans (15oz.) tomato
sauce

2 tsp. sugar
2 lbs. Italian Sausage
1 ½ lbs. Ground Beef (For meatballs)

Line the bottom of a saucepan with oil. Add chopped garlic and onion and sausage and sauté until lightly browned. Put tomatoes in blender and puree. Add to pan and bring to a boil. Then add tomato sauce and remaining spices. Bring to a boil, then simmer covered slightly for 1 hour. Do not simmer too slowly – should be bubbling just slightly. Then take cover off or leave half off, allowing most of the steam to evaporate and cook for 1 ½ hours until sauce reaches desired thickness. (Be careful not to get too thick because sauce will thicken after leaving in refrigerator) (Adjust flavor of sauce with more or less spices according to your taste)

Eggplant Roll-ups

1 large eggplant	¼ cup Parmesan cheese
2 beaten eggs	1 egg
½ cup milk	½ tsp. salt
¼ tsp. salt	¼ tsp. pepper
Olive oil	1 T. chopped parsley
Flour	Spaghetti sauce
1 lb. ricotta cheese	

Peel and slice eggplant lengthwise into ¼ inch thick. Combine egg, milk and salt. Dip each slice of eggplant in flour, then in egg mixture. Cook on both sides in a small amount of hot olive oil until golden brown. Drain on paper towel. Coat 9x13 dish with spaghetti sauce. Combine ricotta, Parmesan cheese, egg, salt, pepper and parsley. Place 1 tablespoon in the cheese mixture in center of eggplant slice. Roll up jellyroll-style. Place seam side down in the 9x13 dish. Cover eggplant with spaghetti sauce. Cover baking dish with tin foil and bake in 350-degree oven for 20-25 minutes or until heated through.

Crescent Spinach and Cheese Bake

¼ cup finely chopped onion
½ clove garlic, minced

2 T. oil
¼ tsp. salt
¼ tsp. pepper

10 oz. pkg. frozen, chopped spinach,

thawed & squeezed to drain

½ cup cooked rice
1 ½ cup shredded mozzarella cheese
2 eggs, slightly beaten
2 T. milk
8 oz. can crescent dinner rolls
3 T. grated parmesan cheese

Heat oven to 350. Grease 9-inch round cake pan. In small skillet, cook onion and garlic in oil until tender. Stir in salt and pepper. Remove from heat. In medium bowl, combine spinach, rice, 1 cup mozzarella cheese, Parmesan cheese, egg, and milk. Stir in onion mixture. Separate dough into 8 triangles. Place 1/3 cups spinach mixture on shortest side of each triangle. Roll up, starting at shortest side of triangle, gently wrapping dough around spinach mixture and rolling to opposite point. Place rolls point side down in prepared pan. Bake at 350 for 25-30 minutes. Remove from oven. Sprinkle with remaining ½ cup mozzarella cheese. Return to oven. Bake 5 minutes longer or until cheese is melted and rolls are golden brown.

Pizza Casserole

2 lbs. Italian sausage	2 (16 oz.) bags mozzarella cheese
1 ½ lbs. small shells	Approx. ½ gallon spaghetti sauce

Remove sausage from casing and brown in oil slightly. Add sauce. Cook sauce and sausage until sausage is cooked. Cook noodles al dente and drain well. In large casserole, layer ingredients, starting with sauce and sausage first, then shells, then sauce and sausage, then cheese. Repeat until all ingredients are used, ending with cheese. Cover with tin foil. Bake in 350 oven for 45 minutes.

Ziti Bake

1 (48 oz.) jar Ragu
1 (16 oz.) pkg. ziti or mostaccioli
1 lb. ground beef
1 (15 oz.) container Ricotta cheese
½ cup grated Parmesan cheese
1 (8 oz.) pkg. shredded mozzarella
cheese

1/8 cup parsley flakes
1 egg, slightly beaten
¾ tsp. salt
¼ tsp. pepper

Cook mostaccioli al dente and set aside. Brown ground beef about 10 minutes and drain grease. Preheat oven to 350. Stir ground beef, ricotta cheese, parmesan cheese, parsley flakes, egg, salt and pepper, and half the sauce together. Add mostaccioli and toss gently to coat well. Spoon mixture into 13x9 baking dish. Pour remaining sauce evenly over mixture. Sprinkle with mozzarella cheese. Bake 20 minutes until hot and bubbly. (Note: I mix the ricotta, eggs, parsley and parmesan cheese together first. I also found it better not to add mozzarella cheese until later.) Cover mixture, heat for 20-30 minutes, then uncover and sprinkle the mozzarella cheese on top and put back into oven until cheese melts.

Meat Filled Shells

1 lb. ground round
½ tsp. onion powder
¼ tsp. garlic powder
2 tsp. parsley
½ tsp. salt
½ tsp. pepper

4 cups prepared red sauce
1 T. grated Romano cheese
1 egg
1 (16 oz.) shredded mozzarella
1-lb. box large shells

Cook shells al dente, drain well and lay each shell on wax paper. Sauté ground round with onion powder, garlic powder, parsley, salt, and pepper. Drain excess grease. Add ½ cup sauce and Romano cheese. Let cool slightly, then add egg and ¼ cup mozzarella cheese. Mix well. Fill shells with meat mixture. In a 9x13 pan, spread a layer of sauce, then fill pan with stuffed shells. Put sauce over shells, cover them completely. Then sprinkle mozzarella cheese over top of shells. Cover with tin foil and bake at 350 for 30 minutes.

Cheese Filled Shells

1-lb. box shells
5 lbs. ricotta cheese
4 eggs
4 cups prepared red sauce
1 (16 oz.) bag mozzarella cheese

2 T. chopped parsley
½ c. Parmesan cheese
1 tsp. salt
¼ tsp. pepper

Cook shells al dente, drain well and lay each shell on wax paper. In separate pan, heat sauce until hot. In large bowl, mix ricotta cheese, egg, parsley, Parmesan cheese, ¾ cup mozzarella cheese, salt and pepper until well mixed. In a 9x13 pan, layer bottom of pan with sauce. Fill shells with ricotta cheese mixture and place on sauce in pan. Cover shells with sauce, making sure they are covered completely. Sprinkle mozzarella cheese over top of shells. Cover with tin foil and bake in 350 oven for 30 minutes.

Mom's White Bread or Pizza Dough
(Great Grandma Apicella)

6 cups sifted flour   2 T. shortening
1 cake of yeast   1 T. salt
1 cup milk   2 T. sugar
1 cup cold water

Dissolve the yeast in one-half cup of lukewarm water. Heat, but do not boil, the milk with shortening, salt, and sugar. Add one cup of cold water. This cools the milk to lukewarm. Add the yeast and stir the flour into the liquid. Kneed until smooth and elastic. Set in a warm place and let it rise, about 1½ hours. Dough should be double in bulk. Push down and roll out for pizza. Put the rolled out dough on a slightly greased pan, then let it rise a little. Put your sauce on dough, a little oil, grated Parmesan cheese and a little oregano. Bake in 400-degree oven until crust is brown. Do the same for bread, except after kneading, divide dough into loaves and put in bread pans and let rise another 20 to 30 minutes. Then bake on 400-degree oven.) Cover pans with dish cloth while rising.) Cook until bread is lightly brown in color, approx. 30 to 45 minutes. (Bread will feel hollow when you tap it.)

Pizza Sauce: Put in a pan ¼ cup of oil and a small chopped onion and one clove of chopped garlic. Sauté until brown then add a large can of tomatoes and a small can of tomato paste, 1-teaspoon salt, ¼ teaspoon pepper, ½ teaspoon parsley and ½ teaspoon basil. Cook for about 1 hour or until sauce is the desired consistency. (Either puree can of tomatoes or chop up tomatoes small.)

Note: This recipe was handed down from my mother Catherine Apicella. On Friday evenings, she would make this light pizza since we could not eat meat and she would also make a loaf or two of bread.

Great Grandma Apicella's Apple Slices or Pie

6 to 8 cups apples   ½ cup or more sugar
1 to 1 ½ teaspoon cinnamon   5 or 6 tbsp. flour
½ teaspoon nutmeg

Line bottom of crust with sugar and flour (about 1 teaspoon each). Mix all ingredients and pour into curst. Dab with butter. Prick top with fork and put larger hole in the middle of the pie so that steam may escape. Seal crust with cold water. Bake for 20 minutes on 450-degree oven and 30 to 45 minutes on 375 oven.

Great Grandma Apicella's Pie Crust

2 cups sifted flour   1 teaspoon salt
2/3 cup Crisco   ¼ teaspoon baking powder
1 teaspoon sugar   4 tablespoons water

Chill after rolled. Roll out and put in 8 or 9-inch pie plate. Cook until light brown on 425 oven. Fill with pudding. For fruit pies, cook 2o min. in oven and 375 oven for 30 to 45 minutes.

Chocolate Peanut Clusters

1 package Reese's Peanut Butter Pieces
½ bag of Nestle Chocolate pieces (approx. 6 oz.)
12 oz. Planter's Peanuts (salted or unsalted)

Melt chocolate in microwave or double boiler. Stir to mix chocolates. Pour in the peanuts and mix while hot. Drop by spoonfuls on waxed paper. Freeze to set

Éclair Graham Cracker Cake

1 box graham crackers   9 oz. cool whip
2 boxes French vanilla instant   (Use 9x13 pan)
pudding

Mix pudding as for pie (use only 3 cups milk). Blend in cool whip. Line pan with graham crackers. Pour half of the mixture over crackers, then layer of crackers over pudding. Pour rest of pudding then another layer of crackers.

Frosting:

2 oz. redi blend liquid   3 tbsp. margarine
chocolate
2 tbsp. white Karo syrup   1 ½ cups powdered sugar
1 tsp. vanilla   3 tbsp. milk

Mix all together. Spread on crackers and refrigerate overnight. Note: Put in all 3 tbsp. milk. Frosting will harden.

Cheese Cake

Graham cracker crust   1 tsp. vanilla
2 eggs   2-8oz. pkg. cream cheese ½
                              cup sugar

Beat eggs. Add sugar and mix well. Add cream cheese and vanilla and beat with electric beater until smooth. Pour into graham cracker crust and cook in 375-degree oven for 20 minutes. Cool slightly. Meanwhile stir: 1-pint sour cream, ¼ cup sugar, and 1 tsp. vanilla. Pour and smooth on top of bakes layer. Then bake in 400-degree oven for 10 minutes.

Use 7 ½ x 11 ¾ glass dish. Follow recipe for graham cracker crust on the box of graham cracker crumbs.

Walnut Horn Cookies (Great Grandma Apicella)

1 cup butter
2 cups sifted all-purpose flour
1 egg yolk, slightly beaten

¾ cup sour cream

¾ cup sugar
1 tsp. cinnamon
¾ cup walnuts, finely
chopped

Cut butter into flour as for piecrust. Mix egg yolk and sour cream. Add to flour and mix thoroughly. Divide dough into three portions and chill overnight. Roll each portion on a floured pastry cloth into a circle about 12 inches in diameter. Combine sugar, cinnamon, and nuts. Sprinkle on dough. Cut in 16 wedges. Roll each wedge firmly, starting at outside edge. Bake on ungreased cookie sheet in a 375-degree oven for 20 minutes.

Mom's Pie Crust (Great Grandma Apicella)

2 cups sifted flour	1 tsp. salt
2/3 cup Crisco	¼ tsp. baking powder
1 tsp sugar	4 T. water

Mix flour, sugar, salt, baking powder, and shortening in bowl with fork until crumbly, make sure shortening is mixed in well. Then add water one tablespoon at a time, until it feels like it can be rolled out easily. You may not need all the water or you might need more. (If you put in too much water, crust will be hard to roll out, as it will crumble. So put the least amount of water as possible.) Roll on a piece of wax paper. Sprinkle some flour on wax paper and also some on rolling pin. Put in a 9 or 10-inch pie plate. Flute ends with thumb. Bake until lightly brown on 425 degrees. Fill with pudding. For fruit pies, cook 15 minutes in 450-degree oven and 375 degree oven for 30 to 45 minutes. Note: This recipe was handed down from my mother, Catherine Apicella. Everybody loved my mom's piecrust.

Strawberry and Spinach Salad

1 pint fresh strawberries
2 bunches fresh spinach
½ cup sugar

1 ½ T. minced green onion
½ teaspoon Worcestershire sauce

½ teaspoon paprika
½ cup olive oil
¼ cup balsamic or cider vinegar
1 T. sesame seeds

Wash strawberries under cool running water. Remove caps and set aside to drain. Wash spinach and remove large tough stems. Tear large leaves into small pieces. Drain. In a medium bowl combine remaining ingredients and whisk together. Slice strawberries into halves or quarters and place in a large bowl. Add dry spinach. Pour dressing over all and toss. Make 8 servings.

Peanut Butter Blossoms

1 ¾ cups flour
1 teaspoon soda
2 tablespoons milk
1 teaspoon vanilla
48 milk chocolate kisses

½ cup peanut butter
1 egg ½ teaspoon salt
½ cup sugar
½ cup brown sugar, packed
½ cup margarine

Combine all ingredients except kisses in large bowl. Use mixer at low speed. Shape dough into balls. Roll balls in sugar. Bake at 350 degrees for 12 minutes. Remove from oven, top with a chocolate kiss. Press on firmly. Remove cookies from cookie sheet to cool.

Easy Enchiladas

12 flour tortillas
1 pkg. (1-5/8 oz) enchilada sauce mix
1 lb. ground beef
2 T. instant minced onion or ½ cup chopped onion
2 cups (8 oz) shredded Cheddar or Monterey Jack cheese
¼ cup chopped or slices black olives

Preheat oven to 350. In a medium saucepan, prepare enchilada sauce mix as directed on package. In a large fry pan, brown ground beef and onion. Drain excess fat. Stir ½ cup enchilada sauce into meat mixture. To assemble, dip each tortilla into sauce. Spoon about 2 tablespoons meat mixture and 1-tablespoon cheese down the center of each tortilla. Roll into thirds and place seam-side down in a 13x9 inch-baking dish. When all tortillas are assembled, pour remaining sauce over top. Sprinkles with olives and extra cheese. Cover with foil. Bake at 350 for 20 minutes.

Chicken Enchiladas

12 flour tortillas
1 pkg. Enchilada sauce mix
4 cooked chicken steaks, cut in small pieces
1 small can (6 oz) tomato paste (plus 1 can tomato sauce, small)
2 cups (8 oz) grated cheddar cheese
3 cups of water

In a saucepan, combine Enchilada mix, 1 can tomato paste and 3 cups of water. Blend well. Bring to a boil; reduce heat. Simmer, uncovered 15 minutes stirring occasionally. Set aside.

In a skillet, warm cut up chicken steaks and ¾ cup sauce. Stir in 1 cup grated cheddar cheese. Pour ½ cup sauce in 13x9 inch baking dish. Coat 12 flour tortillas with remaining sauce. (I dip them in sauce)

Place some chicken mixture in center of each coated tortilla. Roll up and place seam down in baking dish. Pour remaining sauce over enchiladas. Top with 1 cup grated cheddar cheese. Bake, covered at 350 for 30 minutes.

AUG · 62

Grandma & Grandpa Apicella.

Family Gathering at Grandma Apicella's House.

Philip L.   Tommy   Marco L.

Catherine, Tom & GRANDMA APICELLA

Thomas - Mary Lou   Catherine

Connie & Mary Lou

Susie Ann (Sue Ann) DeLuca Bement

Both my grandparents came from Italy. My paternal Grandfather Andrea DeLuca came from Abruzzi, Italy to Chicago Heights, Illinois in the early 1900s. He worked at Inland Steel his entire life. When financially stable he built a two story, brick house on 22nd Street in Chicago Heights, along with all the other immigrants from Abruzzi. All the men that worked at Inland Steel Mill came from the same town in Italy. Pictures of potential brides were sent from Abruzzi and my Grandfather picked my Grandmother Assunta Ricchuito. When she came to the United States they were married.

My paternal grandparents had three children. My father Pasquale (1908-1993) was the oldest, and then they had Ida (1909-2002) and Albert (1922-1978). All three children were born in the United States. My Aunt Ida married Nick Salvucci, who worked at the macaroni factory in Steger. Mr. D'Amico, the owner of the macaroni factory hired Italian immigrants. Unfortunately, my Uncle Nick was killed by injuries sustained in a car accident, when hit by a drunk driver, in 1948. My Aunt Ida remarried Pasquale DiTola, a widower himself. They had one child, a daughter, Elga.

My maternal Grandfather and Grandmother were from Messino, Italy. Pietro Guzzo (1882-1953) and Filomena (Aprile) Guzzo (1890-1964). They were married in Sicily and had six children. While living in Italy, they owned and operated a farm. The first two sons, Peter (1909-1986) and Russell (1912-2007) were born in Italy and the other four children; all females were born in the United States. My mother, Anna DeLuca (1913-2009), Josephine Ruggeri (born 1918), Frances Mikolajczyk (1921-1998), and Angelina Marks (born 1926). My mother and her siblings blessed my Grandparents with sixteen grandchildren. Peter Jr., Phillip, Robert, Russell, Rosanna, Sue Ann, Andrew, Pasquale Jr., Peter, David, Louis, Darlene, Cesar, Georgie, Monica, and Frankie.

My Grandmother, Filomena, inspired me. She started hosting the Feast of the Assumption, which is August 15th. In front of her home on Butler Street, on the east side of Chicago Heights, among her rose garden was the statue of the blessed mother. I called my grandmother "ma". A group of friends and family would gather in front of my grandparent's house to say the rosary in Italian. Every year the celebration would grow. First a weekend, then a week, eventually the entire month turned into a neighborhood celebration. The festivities included prayer, food, and fireworks. I was told a cousin of hers started the feast in Joliet. This year will mark the seventh year of organizing the St. Joseph's table, an old Sicilian tradition at St. Jude's church in New Lenox.

My parents were both first generation born in the United States. My aunt told me my mother was conceived in the "old country".

My father, Pasquale DeLuca (1908-1993) and my mother Anna (1915-2009) were married on June 11, 1939. My father worked in a steel mill, like his father. My mother stayed home and raised her children. I remember her making and selling Linko (bleach). They had a total of five children, four of which were born in five years. I am the eldest child and only daughter, I was born on March 10, 1940. My brothers are Andrew (born 1941), Pasquale (born 1943), Peter (1944-2007), and David (1950). David was born ten years after me; I was like a second mother to him. We gave my parents seven grandchildren Michele, Michael, Tina, Julie, Suzanne, Andrew, and Christmas, and four great grandchildren Cazden, Rhylen, Brookelen, and Greysen.

Times were simple. Everything was homemade. We did not have hot water, we had to boil it. We took baths once a week on Saturday and washed daily by the kitchen sink. A coal furnace generated the heat in our home, we had an icebox and ice was delivered often to help keep food fresh. We went to the store everyday to buy fresh ingredients to make our meals. My father took us hunting in the woods now known as Park Forest he would trap and shoot animals for us to eat. I remember butchering and cleaning rabbits, sparrows, chickens, and pheasants. We had a pet dog named Dego Legs. We had a goat, which provided us with milk and from that we made cheese. We also had chickens in the shed that provided us with fresh eggs. We had two gardens, one on the backyard and one by my Grandfather Guzzo's house by the railroad tracks. My grandfather and father dug two wells to water their gardens. They build sheds to keep the garden tools in. We gathered as a family daily. In the summertime, we spent time in the garden or would visit with our Grandmother who lived down the street. Our family made their own wine. All the homes in the area had basements to keep the wine cool. We had a wine press in our basement; my siblings and I assisted my father when he made the wine. We were members of San Rocco Church in Chicago Heights. My family was very religious and attended mass every Sunday. Mass was said in Latin or Italian. The women wore hats or scarves to cover their heads out of respect for God and the church. Family was an integral part of our lives, neighborhoods were segregated by nationalities, people got along because we all valued the same things and had the same customs. Our Italian neighborhood was known as "The Hill" or "Hungry Hill". The neighborhood was always filled with the scent of fresh baked bread or gravy (tomato sauce). We made our own pasta.

Our family really didn't have a lot of money; we didn't have unemployment in those days. You learned to live on what you made. My dad would go on strike for three to four months. We made ends meet; it was always an honest living. My father was approached to join the Mafia, but he never did.

My father had an eighth grade education and my mother finished through her sophomore year of high school. This was unprecedented during this time. My parents valued education all five of their children graduated high school. I attended a year of college, and then went to beauty school. All four of my brothers were in the military. Andrew and David earned their Associates Degrees. Pasquale, Jr. and Peter, went to barber school, but worked in the field for a short period of time, because men began to wear their hair long. Both were employed by the City of Chicago Heights. All their grandchildren attended college and most obtained college / graduate degrees. My daughter Michele (Bement) McGinn was the first DeLuca grandchild to attend college.

My husband Michael Bement, Sr. (born 1941) and I were married on October 25, 1965. We have three wonderful children. When we were first married, we lived in Dwight, Illinois. We moved back to Chicago Heights and lived there until 1979, when we moved to New Lenox, where we still live today. My husband worked for New Lenox State Bank,

Joliet Federal, and Amerifed. He has his own tax preparation business, which he established in 1967. I worked from our home as a hair stylist while raising our three children. When our youngest child was in second grade, I began working at St. Joseph's Hospital in Joliet, part time. I was always involved with my children's activities. I served as a room mother for 16 years in the Glenwood and New Lenox School Districts. I kept busy taking my children to their extracurricular activities including football, baseball, swimming, band, scouts, and dance lessons. In addition to this, I met with my parents at least once a week for lunch and shopping. We had a cottage in Momence on the Kankakee River, where we spent our weekends as a family. We entertained family and friends there.

There was always a celebration in the works. I threw parties for my children for all of their accomplishments and sacraments. The children were given birthday parties every year until the age of eighteen.

Our first-born child, Michele, was born in 1966. She graduated from Lincoln Way High School on 1984 and Illinois State University in 1988. She worked in the field of social services and is now in the field of education. She married Gary McGinn in May of 1998. They have provided care to over seventeen foster children. They live in Minooka, Illinois.

Michael was born in 1968. He graduated from Lincoln Way High School in 1986; he attended Joliet Junior College and enrolled on the Navy. He was honorably discharged due to hearing loss. He married Vianey Sanchez in October 1998. Michael is self-employed and has a successful pool and pool table installation business. They have four children together, Cazden, Rhylen, Brookelen, and Greysen. They live in Manhattan, Illinois.

Suzanne was born in 1973. She graduated from Lincoln Way High School, Joliet Junior College (1995), Eastern Illinois University (1998), and completed her Master's in Educational Leadership from Aurora University in 2002. She is a special education coordinator and adjunct instructor at the college. She is a life long learner, always taking classes. She married James Withrow in 2003. They live in Joliet, Illinois.

Once I retired, my husband and I have done some traveling. I have been very involved in our parish, St. Jude of New Lenox. In the Council of Catholic Women, I have served as the treasurer for three years and as president for four years. My greatest personal accomplishment in the church was organizing the St. Giuseppe's Table. I am involved with the life of the Holy Spirit organization and also serve as a host. I plan four trips a year to various destinations for the seniors of the parish. I am a hostess at a local restaurant, Papa Joe's, twice a week and enjoy spending time with my family, friends, and grandchildren.

I have always dreamed of going back to the old country. In 2010, I celebrated a milestone birthday. My family threw a surprise party for me. Over 130 people attended from seven states. Later that year, my dream came true. My youngest daughter, Suzanne Bement-Withrow and I traveled to Italy for a trip of a lifetime. We went to numerous cities all over the country in sixteen days. We arrived in Rome, the Eternal City where we met our tour guide. We went to St. Peter's Basilica, the Coliseum, the Forum, Circus Maximus, and Sistine Chapel. We viewed Michelangelo's artistic masterpieces. We traveled to Florence, rode a gondola in Venice, visited the fishing village of Murano. We visited the Church of St. Apollinaris in Classe near Ravenna, and St. Francis' Basilica in Assisi. We visited the city of Pompeii that was buried by the volcanic eruption of Mt. Vesuvius. We visited Naples and took a ferry overnight to Sicily. We visited Palermo, the summit of Mount Pellegrino where we saw the grotto of Santa Rosalia. We drove along the coastal highway and visited the quaint medieval village of Cefalu. We saw the Dorian Temples and Acropolis in Selinunte. We visited Agrigento, Taormina, and the breathtaking Isle of Capri. The trip was more than I expected. It was truly amazing to see the beautiful country my family is from and stand in such a historically rich land. Everything was breathtaking, the sights, sounds, and smells. All of the food was fantastic, the wine flowed freely and friendships of a lifetime were developed. I am proud to be an Italian-American.

Here are some of my favorite recipes:

Sue's Italian Round Steak Stew

Ingredients:

3-4 lbs. of round steak, cut in 1-1 ½ inch cube
6 tablespoons of olive oil
1 medium onion, chopped
4 cloves of garlic
1/5 tablespoons of salt
¼ teaspoon black pepper
6 large carrots, sliced
Parsley, chopped
4 stalks of celery, sliced
2 Bouillon cubes
4 cups hot water
1 cup dry red wine (optional)
6 medium potatoes, quartered
1 medium green pepper, cut into 1-inch pieces
1 large can of tomatoes

In a large stockpot, brown meat, garlic, and chopped onions in olive oil until meat is browned. Add parsley, salt, pepper, carrots, and celery. Allow steaming for about 15-20 minutes. Blend Bouillon cubes and water and pour into kettle with wine. Bring to a boil; reduce heat, cover, and cook slowly about 1 ½ hours. Add remaining vegetables and cook gently about ½ hour more or until meat and vegetables are tender. Gravy will be thin; it may be thickened with flour, if desired. Serves six.

Italian Meatballs

Ingredients:

5 lbs. of ground round
¼ lb. ground veal

3 tablespoons fresh parsley, minced
1 cup Romano Imported Cheese
2 teaspoons pepper

1 cup milk

½ lb. ground pork
1 cup Italian Breadcrumbs
5 eggs
4 teaspoons salt
3-4 cloves of garlic, minced

Mix well. Brown in olive oil; turn to brown on all sides. Remove from skillet, cook in Spaghetti Gravy for one hour (marinara sauce).

Italian Ricotta Easter Pie

Filling Ingredients;

1 pound white raisins (soak until plump), washed and drained
3 pounds ricotta cheese
2 large eggs, slightly beaten
1 ¾ cups of sugar
4 oz. chopped citron (optional)

In a large bowl, beat eggs. Add sugar, citron, raisins, and ricotta cheese. Mix ingredients well and set aside. This is the filling.

Pastry;

½ cup scalded milk   dash of salt
3 eggs, beaten   2 cups of sugar
3 Tablespoons, anise seed   1 teaspoon baking powder
4-6 cups of flour (enough to make dough soft/dough fall off your hands)
¾ stick margarine or butter, melted and cooled

Beat eggs in bowl. Add sugar, milk (cooled off), margarine, anise seed, baking powder, and salt. Add sifted flour slowly and mix well. (Dough should be like piecrust). Work dough on floured board until smooth. Roll out to fit butter, greased and floured 17x1x1 inch cookie sheet. Next, spoon in the ricotta filling evenly and seal with remaining pastry. Flute edges like piecrust. Beat together one egg yolk and two tablespoons of milk. Brush the top of the crust evenly. With wet fork, pierce pastry dough through to keep the dough from rising while baking (about one inch a part). Bake in preheated oven for 55-60 minutes until golden in color. Make the day before serving.

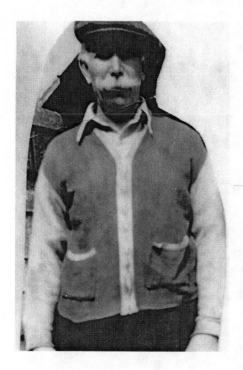

My Grandmother, Filomena (Aprile) Guzzo

My mother, Anna Guzzo in front of Bloom High School, Chicago Heights, Illinois

The Guzzo Family

Back Row: Peter, Francis, Josephine, & Russell
Front Row: Pietro, Sr., Angelina, Anna, and Filomena

Pasquale DeLuca, 1926

Mr. & Mrs. Pasquale DeLuca
June 11, 1939
St. Rocco Church
Chicago Heights, Illinois

Backyard of the house on "The Hill"

Front Row: Andrew & Sue Ann
Back Row: Paquale holding Pasquale, Jr. & Anna holding Peter

Anna & Pasquale
Sue, Andrew, & Pasquale, Jr.

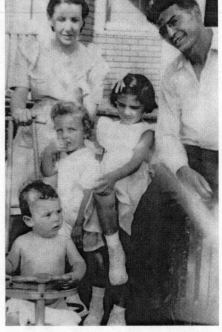

Michael Bement, Sr. & Sue Ann (DeLuca) Bement

The DeLuca Children

Front Row: David & Peter
Middle Row: Andrew & Pasquale
Back Row: Sue Ann

Front Row: Michael, Sr. & Sue Ann
Back Row: Michele, Michael, Jr. and Suzanne

The Bement Grandchildren

Greysen, Cazden, Rhylen & Brookelen

Christmas 2011

Annette Stella Dixon

This story has been told many times in movies, daily soap operas, in books and lately on Television. This is not an unusual story, but it is my story. My mother at the time of my birth was Rose DeChristopher, married to Louis DeChristopher. She was abused by my biological father and was eventually divorced. The divorce took place five months after I was born, since my mother was granted full custody of me, she accepted no child support from him and did not want him to contact us.

When I was two, my mother said that my father, mother and I went to visit his mother because she wanted to see her only grandchild. I never saw her again. At age three, I remember my father bringing me a gold locket, that I still have today and a box of Valentine Candy. He continually searched for us and was able to find us, since my mother was still a single mother and did not change her name. The last time I saw him, I was four years old and my stepfather asked him not to come and see me because he wanted to adopt me. That was the last time I saw him. My uncle said he saw him many times, asking people where my mother and I lived, but didn't know our last name. He searched for me when I was in St. Martin Commercial and I didn't find out about it because my mother told me years later. Father Millan who was a priest at the time notified my mother that my biological father was asking about me. He was shocked because there were no records of my being adopted. I was told never to tell anyone that I was adopted because this man would harm us if he knew where we were located. It was also around this time that my maternal grandmother was visited by Louis DeChristopher. He found her through an obituary, contacted the funeral director and visited her. He said he wanted to see his daughter. She said she would not give an address, but if he had a letter, she would give it to her. So she did after asking my mother if it was all right to do so. I read the letter so many times trying to decide the right thing to do. Should I see him or not.

Within that letter, Louis stated that his mother was sick and she wanted to see me. I analyzed the letter and realized this man was either ignorant, or insane. He jumped from wanting to see his little baby to be sure to bring your mother. I was sure it was my mother he wanted to see and not so much me. After hearing my father, John Stella and my mother talking in bed one evening, I knew then that I should not see him. I contacted the number he had left and gave a message to his relative to give to Louis. We were never contacted by him again. So I carried this secret once again. When my husband and I adopted our daughter Michelle, my adoption was discussed with our counselor in the sessions we had at the Chicago Foundling Home in order to apply for adoption for an infant.

I have only one regret and that is that I did not get to see my grandmother again. Twice in my life I decided to search for my biological family. In 1981, I went to Father Lane at Holy Family Church and he gave me the name and address of Mario DeChristopher. Mario had the tobacco and newspaper store on Taylor Street, just a few businesses east of Racine. He was very receptive to me until I showed him a picture of Louis and my mother's wedding photo. He turned cross and said I don't want to talk to you again, goodbye. I was hurt and taken back by his attack on me, but I dismissed it as an insult against my father, Louis DeChristopher, and did not take it personally against me. It taught me not to look any further into Louis DeChristopher's heritage or genealogy. It was at that point in my life, my father John Stella meant more to me than anyone else in my life. I thought of all the kindness that he gave to me and forgot about all my teenage bitterness that I had toward him.

In 1996, I searched for my biological father once again. I found his records including his social security records; he died in 1993 in DuQuoin, Illinois. I had his death certificate and on it was listed many facts of birth, names of parents, and last place of residence. He was in a nursing home, got sick and brought to the hospital, died there and buried at Sunset Memorial Park Cemetery in DuQuoin on December 22, 1993. There was a funeral for him, which I found out the nursing home provided the service. I contacted the administrator of the Fairview Nursing Center and she informed me that Kim Dorsey was the activity director and knew my father. Kim found pictures of him, but nothing else. She had purchased a pocket watch and wondered where it had disappeared. There was a box, she said put away for him when he died. But after the years didn't know where it went.

Kim wrote a nice letter in 1997 stating that she was sorry that she didn't know he had a child. It would have been so nice for him to have family, for he didn't have visitors. They would send letters but they were always returned and the last letter they had sent stated, please do not send anything at this address again. She seemed to enjoy him and his brief stories. He talked about living in Chicago and being a gunman for Al Capone. He told many stories, but the staff did not believe him. He even said he was married once for a very short time, but didn't say he had a child.

I didn't expect him to ever mention me since I left a message long ago to his relative stating that I had a father who loved me and was good to me and asked him the question "ask Louis DeChristopher where has he been for 15 years of my life". I remember the man replying, "I can't answer that, it's up to him to tell you. Give me your phone number and he will call you". I said, "No, I have a father who is with me all the time. Tell him I said Goodbye".

The administrator told me that my father was in Manteno State Hospital from 1960 until 1967 when it closed down. He was then transferred to a mental facility in Anna, IL and stayed there until 1977, when they were warehousing mental patients into nursing homes. He remained in the nursing home until his death in 1993, he was 81 years old. He was the last family member to die.

In August 2007, I was in Johnson Bowman Center at Rush Hospital and I met a woman the day before I was to leave the rehab facility. Her name was Della C. Fosco and she had mentioned that she lived at Polk and Bell Street. I don't know why I asked, but I did ask her if she knew the DeChristopher family on Flournoy and Kedzie St. She said she was related to the DeChristopher family. I dismissed it with I don't think that would be the same DeChristopher family. Then she said you're right, when I told her the names of Louis's mother and father. She said your grandmother and my mother were best of friends. She also told me that my grandfather was not too nice, he was introverted and moody, but my grandmother made up for it, for she was so friendly and smiley and a wonderful person. She mentioned my grandmother died in 1965 and buried at Mount Carmel Cemetery. I never heard from Della again, so I went to her house and found out she had died three months after I had left the hospital. Della was taken from Johnson Bowman to Villla Scalabrini to live out the rest of her life.

In 2009, after recuperating from the double knee replacements, I decided to go to Mount Carmel Cemetery to find where the grandparents and aunt were buried. My mother mentioned that Louis had a sister that died in childbirth. What a new awakening I had regarding this family. My mother gave me information that Louis had given her, for she hadn't met the mother or his siblings prior to the wedding. She mentioned to me that she did not meet his immediate family but he took her to an uncle's house and cousins home to introduce her to them. The only time she met the mother was when we all went together in 1945. My mother said she was a very thin, tiny woman and appeared to be old. She couldn't speak English, but my father knew English and Italian and translated for them. A story I thought was odd was the grandmother wanted to give me money and Louis said no she doesn't need it. My mother could understand a little Italian but not speak it. She also said that there were two other people visiting at the time we were there. A brother in the Army, for he had his uniform on and an elderly gentleman who my mother thought was her male friend. When my mother asked Louis about him, he said no they're just friends. I wondered about his remaining family and whether they had children and did I have relatives. Needless to say I was going to find out more after searching more records and looking up death certificates.

After going to Mount Carmel Cemetery, I first asked for Nicola DeChristopher because he was the first to die. When they checked his records, they told me that Florence DiCristofano paid for three graves in 1933 when they were burying Nick DeChristopher. Well after many months and looking through death certificates of these people, the 1930 Census and the Draft paper, I had the whole picture. Nicola DiCristofano was married to Filomena and in 1918 lived at 1037 West 11th St. Nicola came from Pizzone, Italy on the Massilia Ship, docked in Naples and arrived in New York on May 22, 1905. He was age 23, single at that time. He was with sixteen others from the same town and his relatives were Vincenzo, 16 and Pietro DiCristofano, 32. I do not know when Filomena and Nicola married, but I do know that they had a daughter Antoinette in 1908, Peter, 1909, Louis 1912, Carolo, 1914 and Dominick, 1916. Nicola worked digging sewers in the Harrison and Canal Tunnelsl By 1933, they had a brick three flat at 3239 West Flournoy and a tragedy took place that year. An accident occurred while Nicola was up on a light post changing a globe on the light. The death certificate showed that there was an investigation and death was declared an accident.

In 1938, Antoinette DeChristopher Korous died from Chronic Nephritis due to Toxemia of pregnancy. Death of fetus due to toxemia. This information was on the death certificate and Peter DiCristofano was the listed informant for Nicola and Antoinette's death certificate. The husband was James Korous and they had owned a home at 2930 48th Court, Cicero, IL. She was almost 30 and was buried in one of the graves purchased in 1933. Searching through many other records, I found that Peter is buried at Mount Carmel Cemetery and died June 22, 1962. Filomena, now called Florence died February 8, 1965 and buried in the third grave with Nicola and Antoinette. I have pictures of the three deceased and the tombstone and gravesite in which they are buried.

In 1965 Dominick was the informant for Florence, they lived at 1549 North Leamington. The funeral took place at St. Peter Canisius Church. There is no mention of Caralo as to where he died and was buried. After receiving the death certificates of Peter, who passed away in June 1962, buried at Mount Carmel Cemetery and Dominick died in 1981. I was able to check the grave of Dominick at Queen of Heaven Cemetery, who obviously married at a late age and after his mother passed away. On Dominick's death certificate was listed his wife's name, Margaret Laughlin Harty. When I check Dominick's grave, the office of Queen of Heaven Cemetery has Dominick's last name as DeChristopher but on the tombstone it written as Dicristofano. Margaret, Dominick's wife dies much later and on her obituary lists Margaret's first husband, deceased James Hary, then Dominick DeChristopher, deceased, buried at Queen of Heaven, across the road from Mount Carmel Cemetery. When I visited the graves, I noticed that DiCristofano was engraved on the marker as Dominick and Margaret DiCristofano. There were no DeChristopher or Dicristofano children listed in the obits, but there were 8 Harty children, six living and 31 grandchildren, 54 great grandchildren and 7 great great grandchildren. So it appears that I was the only grandchild of Mr. and Mrs. Nicola DiCristofano and the family genes within me will be lost at my demise. Genealogy is interesting in many ways for it was through Dominick Candeloro's oral history of the Pizzonesi in Chicago that gave me the incentive to look into the lives of a family I never knew but hold their genes.

In order to get to know one's self, we need to acquire an interest in our ancestors. How well we get to understand and learn about our heritage and ethnic being is to look into the past and study our family history. In my case, I had to seek out the people who were deceased for I don't have any living relatives in my DiCristofano immediate family, but there may be some DiCristofano cousins still alive. By doing this, I started to learn a little about genealogy, as I studied about my relatives from the past. The word genealogy means a chart of recorded history of the descent of a person or family from an ancestor or ancestors. About the oral history of the immigrant from Pizzone, the study is about the people who immigrated from Molise who have identified themselves as Abruzzese. Molise was submerged in that region of Abruzzo, therefore calling themselves an Abruzzese. Transportation routes appear to link Pizzone with Castel di Sangro more efficiently than with its current provincial capital of Isernia, which had earthquake destruction several years ago.

Pizzone is a small town 724 meters above sea level in the northeast corner of Molise, near the borders of Abruzzo, Lazio, and Campania. Names for the characteristic large peak above the town, "Pizzone" is just a few kilometers from Castel San Vincenzo with whose inhabitants the Pizzonesi have had a great deal of interaction both in Italy and in Chicago.

Pizzonese immigrant to Chicago were aided and encouraged by two related phenomena: access to the Hod Carriers Union (later referred to as the Laborers' International Union, and the rise of independent sewer contractors among Pizzonese paesani. The first development relates closely to the career of Peter Fosco. Born of Pizzonesi parents in Russia in 1894, Fosco immigrated to Chicago in 1913. In 1915 he became the business agent for the hod carriers union. It seems logical that the large number of Chicago Italians, especially Abruzzese (including Molisani) in the ranks of unskilled construction laborers contributed to Fosco's early success as did his relationship by marriage to hod carrier and sewer tunnel union leaders Joseph and Anthony D'Andrea. Fosco became a citizen in 1918 and unsuccessfully ran for the U.S. Congressman from the first district. In that same year he became president of Local #2 of the Laborers Union in which office he serve until 1936 when he became regional head of the national.

Again through knowledge of this oral report, I was able to piece together the acquaintance of DiCristofano Family (Nicola and Filomena) The D'Andrea Family, (Della Fosco's maiden name) and the Peter Fosco family again Della's Husband's father and husband. And through all of these names realize how they all arrived on the Massilia Ship in May 22, 1905 and Nicola worked for Green and Sons in 1918 digging for sewers at the Harrison and Canal Tunnel. I believe in piecing every detail and document of Nicola and Filomena's life, thanks to Della Fosco, I will be able to share this knowledge with the Pizzonese in Chicago.

The conclusion of the oral history from Pizzone gave me the inspiration to further my interest to search for my roots in Molise-Abruzzo regions. Ancestry will help me to culminate my discovery about the other half.

The Pizzonesi in Chicago (Oral History taken from online Casa Italia Dominic Candeloro, Author)

Here are some of my favorite recipes:

Caesar Dressing

Egg Yolks

Parmesan Cheese

Salt, Pepper, and Oregano

Vinegar

Blend and serve slightly chilled

Zucchini

1 T. of olive oil
4 oz. of water
1 clove of garlic
4 oz. of tomato paste

½ tsp. of oregano
1 large zucchini
salt and pepper to taste

Put oil, garlic in pan and fry until tender. Add tomato paste, oregano, water, salt, pepper, and cubed zucchini. Cook until tender. Add cheese and a beaten egg one half hour before done.

Hamburger Parmigiana

2 lbs. ground beef
1 ½ tsp. salt
½ tsp. pepper
1 egg, slightly beaten
3 tsps. Milk
¼ cup chopped onion (optional)

1 C. breadcrumbs
2 T. butter
1-8 oz. tomato sauce
1 C. mozzarella cheese
¼ cup parmesan cheese
1 piece of garlic

Make patties, season with salt and pepper and onions (optional). Dip patties in egg mixed with milk, then into breadcrumbs. Brown patties on both sides in butter. Cook well down, pour tomato sauce over patties, and continue to cook. Remove from heat; top each patty with mozzarella cheese and sprinkle parmesan on top. Broil until cheese is melted. Serves approx. 8.

French Italian Quiche

1 lb. Italian sausage
1 pkg. mozzarella cheese
4 eggs

1 lb. sliced mushrooms
1 cup whipped cream
¼ tsp. salt

Preheat oven to 350 degrees. Bake deep-dish frozen pie shell eight minutes. Use the ten-inch size or prepare your own. Brown sausage and break into small pieces. Remove sausage; boil mushrooms in a large pan for 5 minutes then drain. Combine sausage, mushrooms, cheese, and whipping cream in a large bowl. Add beaten eggs, salt to mixture and mix well. Pour into pastry shell. Bake for 45 minutes. Serve after an hour at room temperature.

LaVerne DePaul White

On January 12, 1927 I made my entrance into the world. On July 14, 1930 my parents were blessed with my twin brothers Frank and Conrad. It was a happy day for us but especially so because the Daily News was giving away a washing machine to any mother who had twins that day. Lucky us!

My high school years were filled with parties and fun. It was especially important to include all the family in the lively celebrations. That way I felt very much a part of our extended family.

In tune with the special Italian trait of compassion for the poor, I remember my mom inviting friends and neighbors to share a meal with us on Sunday. This was especially important during the Depression when so many struggled to keep their families fed. Not only did they share our delicious food but were also entertained with piano music and song. It was easier to get through the week when we could look forward to a Sunday of fun.

In 1945, I graduated from Logwood Academy and continued my education at Chicago Teacher's College since I wanted to teach in the Public School System. Even as I taught I attended DePaul at night. In 1959, my twin brothers and I graduated from DePaul University with our Masters. We served as public school teachers all of our adult lives and so fulfilled our dreams of educating Gods "little" ones.

My entire life has been filled with happy memories but I want to share one of them with you. In 1980, Gloria Gulino Koziek while traveling in Europe made arrangements to visit the Vatican with her husband. Before the mass, Gloria whispered to her husband she wanted to use a washroom. The Bishop, our present Pope Benedict VI, said, "yes, you can use the Pope's washroom." Gloria was ushered to a very large and beautiful room and never tired telling of that amazing experience. Not too many can boast of using the Pope's washroom and of personally being escorted there by the present Pope.

Fifty-five years ago, I married Joseph Edward White. We were blessed with four children, Loretta Ann, Julie Marie, James Martin, and Cecilia Rita. We are very proud of our children and their achievements.

My religious life has always been important to me. As a volunteer in the Alcoholic Outreach, I work closely with couples that need help. As a Pro-Life and Courage Program member, I helped save the lives of many babies. I also taught in the CCD Program and have been a part of the Charismatic movement for thirty-five years.

Presently, I am involved in making known the United Heart of Jesus and Mary Program based in Ohio. I have been very successful in disseminating information even as far as Canada and Japan. I have visited the site three times and have been very impressed. I will do all I can to make information about these holy appearances known and loved.

Here are some of my favorite recipes:

Biscotti Cookies

1 cup butter
6 eggs
½ cups of sugar
2 tsp. Anise extract (Other flavors can be substituted)
5 cups flour
6 tsp. Baking Powder
¼ tsp. of salt
1 cup of chopped almonds (optional)

Heat oven to 400 degrees. Cream butter and sugar in large bowl. Beat in eggs and blend well. Add flavoring of choice (maple, almond, or vanilla, etc.) Add baking powder, almonds (dried cranberry or flavored chips can be substituted) and flour (pudding mix can be added). Knead until smooth. Separate dough into 6 sections. Roll each part into a log, 12 inches long by 1-inch diameter. Place logs on greased baking sheet (or utilize parchment paper), 2 inches apart and flatten slightly with your hand.

Bake at 400 degrees for 15 minutes. Remove, cool, and cut diagonally, ½ inch intervals, into slices. Return the slices on cookie sheet to the oven for 5-10 minutes, until slightly brown.

Cool, apply frosting and ENJOY.

Stuffed Italian Rolls

1.5 lbs. Ground chuck
1 onion, chopped fine
1 tsp. Salt & Pepper
1 can Hunts tomato sauce
1 can chopped black olives
¼ lb. grated American cheese
1 dozen Italian rolls

Mix all ingredients except rolls and cook for 15 minutes. Pull bread out of rolls and stuff with mixture. Wrap individually in foil (may freeze). Bake at 350 degrees for 30-40 minutes. Longer if frozen.

Pasta e Fagioli

1 ¼ tsps. Olive oil
1 cup recipe-ready crushed tomatoes
2 cloves garlic, minced
2 Tbsps. Rosemary, crumbled
4 cups vegetable or chicken stock
2 lbs. canned white kidney beans, rinsed and drained
¼ lb. rotini pasta or fusilli
¾ lb. zucchini, cooked and cut into ½ inch pieces
2 Tbsps. Grated Parmesan cheese

Heat oil in a heavy nonreactive saucepan over medium heat. Add next 3 ingredients. Simmer 5 minutes, stirring occasionally. Add ½ tsp. of the stock. Combine remaining stock with 1-cup kidney beans in a blender. Puree. Transfer to tomato mixture. Add remaining kidney beans. Bring to a boil. Reduce heat to low and simmer 10 minutes. Add pasta and zucchini. Cook 10-12 minutes or until pasta is al dente. Season with salt and pepper to taste. Serve with Parmesan.

BIAGIO
GULINO

Catherine Damico Boyle

My story begins in the late 1950's. My family consisted of five children, my mother, and my father. We were two boys, two girls, and myself. I have the best siblings ever. We fought like crazy when we were young and growing up but I think it was because my mom was so strict that we took out our frustrations on each other. My sister Justine is the oldest; six years older than me. She is the worrier and the mother hen. She was married at eighteen and is still married to the same man, Wayne. They have one daughter, Jill, who is my godchild. In Italian families, and most likely in others, that is an honor. Next is brother Mike, who is five years older than I am. He is married to my sister-in-law Sharon. They have two boys, Mike and Nick. After Mike comes Sam. He is our external fix-it guy, also responsible. Sam has three girls, Stacey, Stephanie, and Gianna. He is single now, but serious with a new girl. Next is me. I am not the black sheep but have caused my family much worry and problems in the past. I am trying to be better. Last but not al all least is my youngest sister Karen, who is six years younger than I am. She is married to Tim, and they have one son, Robert. Karen is a policewoman, very serious about everything but a good sister.

My extended family is quite large; my mom had four siblings and my father had fourteen. On my father's side, I have over one hundred cousins. You can imagine when we get together it is like a sideshow. We are all high strung and communicate in the usual loud and friendly way. We also like to tell each other how to do things. This leads to a noisy but friendly gathering.

I am 100% Italian and very proud of it. My mother's family came from Simbario, Calabria and my father's side came from Sicily. Since each town has its own favorite foods and traditions, I grew up with a very rich Italian cultural background.

I was born on the South Side of Chicago near Chinatown. This was a very Italian neighborhood. My life was immersed in all things Italian and filled me with a deep joy and pride in my heritage.

My church was Santa Maria Incoronata and it adhered very closely to the Italian way of celebrating many religious feast days. In August, we celebrated the feast of St. Rocco and in September, the Feast of the Blessed Mother. I especially love these Italian traditions and they are a treasured memory.

During the processions, I remember the elderly women dressed in black dresses and stockings either walking the whole way or even on their knees as a special sacrifice. They were people of deep faith and very devout. I was always proud to join in these celebrations.

At age five, we moved to the Gage Park neighborhood. It was very different from our Chinatown Italian home. Here we were part of a mixed group of people, mostly Polish. However, we kept all our traditions and attended St. Clare de Montefalco church. I completed my elementary schooling there and had many friends.

Italians celebrate receiving the sacraments in a big way. We had great parties in the basement or in the yard. Since our relatives lived upstairs and my mother was a stay-at-home mother, she and Aunt Connie did a lot of cooking together. Everything was homemade and delicious. The Italian spices made everything very tasty. Our parties were an unforgettable joy.

Besides being a good cook, my mother was constantly cleaning. There was no end to the way she kept everything spotless. It was a trait that rubbed off on her children to the point of making us a little neurotic.

I had a wonderful childhood even though there wasn't a lot of scholastic achievement in our family. My father peddled fruits and vegetables and worked very hard to make a living. His stories made us street smart and that was an asset. He also instilled in us a willingness to work hard for what we wanted to achieve. My father died in 1989.

While I attended Maria High School in 1975, we celebrated the Holy Year by going to Italy. It was a great experience that I cherish. Going through the five holy doors of the Cathedral churches was a highlight of the trip.

In 1995, I married John Boyle and we had one son, Frank. Life went along fairly well and we continued to enjoy my Italian traditions and John's Irish ones. We thought very little about how our lives could change drastically.

My mother contracted Lou Gehrig's and her children rallied to take care of her. She died in April of 2000, and six months later I lost my wonderful husband John. It was a sad time and my faith helped me bear it courageously.

My son has been God's great blessing to me. He teaches me every day to be a better person. He has always been a great student and a pretty serious boy. Well, after losing your father when you are nine, it's hard. He has never done anything to cause me worry and has been very responsible. He is 20 now, going to college and working at UPS. He helps me so much. I now know what unconditional love is.

I want very much to steep my son Frank in the knowledge of his Irish and Italian culture. Because of this, I like to call to mind some of my favorite memories. One of them was that we never ate meat on Fridays. Another was that we only ate fish on Christmas. Meat was not allowed Christmas Day.

Easter was a favorite time of the year because my mother made homemade ravioli. A sheet was places on the bed and my job was to transfer the raw ravioli from the table to the bed. When mom was not looking, I ate a few. When she noticed what was happening, my mother pretended to be mad, but I think she expected this to happen.

Easter was also a time for many church services. We attended these and always looked forward to the Easter bread. This consisted of dough with an egg tucked in a pocket. When this was baked it was a special Easter treat.

My sister and I try to keep all the Italian traditions each year. We can handle most of the food except for the canolli shells. It takes a special talent for that so we go to the Italian bakery for desserts.

They say we never know when the next "thing" will zap us. For me it was in 2008 when I was diagnosed with Non-Hodgkin's Lymphoma. It meant many stays in the hospital, surgeries, and countless trips to the doctor and many days when I wondered how it would all end. I could not have gone through what I did without my brothers, sisters, son, church, neighbors, friends, and co-workers. My siblings pushed me, fed me, massaged, took me to doctors, and organized my appointments. Each one had their own specialty. Thanks to the many prayers and to my faith in my God, I am now in remission and feeling great.

So now you know, I am so very grateful to be Italian. I want my family traditions to be carried out by my son, Frank, and also by my extended family. I can tell that we are doing very well. We follow what mom and dad started, and lovingly remember her as we do so.

Here are some of my favorite recipes:

Famous Stuffed Artichokes

15 medium artichokes
6 cups Italian style breadcrumbs
2 sticks salted butter
1 ½ cups fresh parsley
1 ½ tsp. salt
1 ½ tsp. pepper
1 cup grated parmesan cheese
a couple pinches of oregano and basil
2 tbsp. granulated chicken bouillon

In a large bowl, mix all dry ingredients together except chicken bouillon and butter. Put one medium onion and one bulb of garlic in food processor. Melt butter in large frying pan and add onions and garlic. Sauté until tender. Pour wet mixture over crumb mixture. Mix well, add canola oil until you can put crumbs in palm of hand and they stay together.

Clean artichokes. Cut top and stem. Then go back and clip the tops straight across to get rid of thorns. Use scissors. Next, run cold water over every artichoke and try to open while rinsing. Turn all clean and opened artichokes upside down on paper towel to drain. Put large bowl of crumb mixture in sink and start opening each leaf and fill with your hands. Get a large roasting pan with lid. Line up the artichokes stem down and pack tightly. 14-15 should fit in large roasting pan. Mix 2 tablespoons of chicken bouillon in about 3-4 cups of hot water to make sure they dissolve. Pour water mixture so that there is ¼ to ½ inches covering the artichokes on the bottom. Put lid on. Use both burner front and back medium heat (steam). Every ten minutes take lid off and baste each artichoke. You may have to add more water but no more bouillon. Every batch has a different cooking time, approximately one hour. When you can grab a leaf from the center and pull easily, they are done. Let rest a while.

Low Cal Tiramisu

1 ½ cups cold 2% low fat milk
1-8 oz. Light Philadelphia Cream Cheese
2 tsp. Maxwell House instant coffee
1 tbsp. hot water
2 tbsp. brandy
1 pkg. (4 serving size) Jell-O vanilla sugar free instant pudding and pie filling
2 cups thawed Light Cool Whip topping
1 pkg. (3 oz.) ladyfingers, split
1 square Baker's semi-sweet chocolate (grated)

Place ½ cup of milk and cream cheese in blender. Blend on medium speed until smooth. Dissolve coffee in water, add to blender with brandy and remaining 1 cup of milk. Add pudding mix. Cover and blend until smooth. Pour into bowl and immediately stir in whip topping. Cut ladyfingers in half horizontally, cover bottom of springform pan with ladyfinger halves. Place remaining halves, cut ends down around sides of pan. Spoon pudding mixture into pan. Refrigerate 3 hours or until firm. Remove sides of pan. Garnish with chocolate. Serves 12.

From left myself, brother Mike brother John sister Christine sister Karen (2009)

Myself and Mom

My Dad

Brother Mike, Myself and Dad (1977)

My Husband John and Son Frank (1992)

Myself as a new mother at Mom's house in Las Vegas (1992)

Mom with son Frank
in 1992

Frankie's other Gram
(Delores) 1992

Myself, My husband
John and son
Frankie as Mom
in Las Vegas
in 1995

Francine Lanzillotti Lazzara

My earliest childhood educational memories are of Seton and Alcuin Montessori Schools. I was too young at the time (3 to 9 years) to understand how their system of education differed from the norm but I was aware of the emphasis they put on independence.

The methods used were the brainchild of Maria Montessori, a famous Italian educator who was years ahead of her time. She believed children learned through exploration, manipulation and communication. All these led to developed power of reasoning, imagination and creativity.

My sister Angela and I attended 3 Montessori schools up to the 5th grade. The last school, located in Maywood, was by far the most unique. It was a Frank Lloyd Wright Mansion on an acre of land complete with a beautiful grotto, multiple greenhouses and live sheep. My fondest memory is stomping grapes to make red wine and baking unleavened bread in preparation for my First Holy Communion.

My parents worked hard to send my older sister and I to private schools and encouraged us to appreciate the diversity exposed to us at a very young age.

My parents were just as passionate about family traditions as education. Feast days and Sundays were special occasions in our Italian household. The tradition was as follows: Attend Sunday Mass, while the pot of "gravy" was simmering. It was impossible to pass by that pot without dipping a piece of Italian bread. Nearby, one of the many relatives was preparing the salad, someone else was checking on the other pasta dishes while others were setting multiple tables for the many guests.

Since my father, Joe Lanzillotti was an attorney and Mayor of Berwyn, he often received gifts of homemade red wine, dried salami and prosciutto which were a delicious appetizer to our meal.

We lived in a bungalow and of course had a finished basement with a full kitchen to accommodate our large extended family. Even those not related by blood were considered family and welcomed to drop in anytime. Everybody enjoyed the loud afternoons full of music (piano, accordion, and or ukulele) and lots of laughter.

After the meal, the aprons would go back on to clean in preparation for dessert and a long night of card playing. My mom and dad still have jars full of coins lined up along a basement window.

My father was one of the original four founders of the Italian American Club of Berwyn in 1966. My mother, Rosemary Lanzillotti, has always been an active member of the Ladies Auxiliary Club (Secretary). This club continues to be an important part of Berwyn's rich history.

My favorite memories are from the annual I.A.C.O.B picnic where everyone wore red, white, and green. There was non-stop food, music, dancing, raffles, games, and races for all ages. Bocci ball, Baseball. Softball, 3-legged races, water balloons, and egg tossing for the brave. Again, Italian food was central, from pepper and egg sandwiches for breakfast to sausage and Italian beef sandwiches for lunch to Italian ice for dessert.

In 2010, the I.A.C.O.B. honored my father as "Man of the year" at their annual raffle and dinner dance. It was another memorable evening of music, laughter, good friends, and of course delicious food beginning with my dad's favorite appetizer, cold fish salad. In addition, the annual event raises money for scholarships and offers chances to win cash prizes (a Cadillac raffle).

I should have know my fate was to meet and marry an Italian man, even after leaving Berwyn and attending college in Davenport, Iowa.

In 1981, after graduating from Nazareth Academy I met Chuck Lazzara at St. Ambrose College (now a university). Not only did my Uncle Carmie Lanzillotti (my Dad's twin) attend the college, my father graduated from St. Ambrose in 1950. Chuck and I graduated in 1985, wed in 1987 and moved into our current home of 26 years in Evergreen Park. Our children, Taylor Ann is 24 years old, and working towards her Master's Degree in Art Therapy at Adler School of Psychology. Our son, Julian Joseph is 22 years old and finishing up his Business Undergrad at St. Ambrose University before continuing on to Culinary School.

Taylor and Julian attended St. Bernadette grade school where our family was fortunate to meet Sr. Mary Ventura. She is quite a unique person and dedicated Dominican Nun who's been teaching over 60 years. She has the same effect on young and old. At first glance you are intimidated by dark eyes and full habit but after spending time with her you realize how caring and humble she is. To this day I don't think she realizes how many lives she has touched.

Even though I was busy working, traveling, and volunteering at church and school, I could never say "no" to Sr. Mary. In 1998 she formed an Italian American Women's Club and asked if I would drive her to the Oak Lawn Library where our 1st meeting was held. When I opened the car door to let Sr. Mary out, she said, "Aren't you coming in?"

It's been 14 years and I'm still in, in fact, I'm currently the President of the club. We've had our challenges and sadness with club members illnesses and death but we're also formed a bond of sisterhood that can't be broken. We've all committed to the mission statement. Even though the members are from different generations and have taken different paths in life we have never forgotten why we joined – to empower and encourage the next generation of Italian Americans to be proud of their rich heritage and to continue to live very fulfilling lives just like our Italian ancestors.

The Italian American Women's Club has written and published 2 books allowing us to give over $12,000.00 in scholarships to Italian American students looking to further their education. To say that we're "small but mighty" pretty much sums us up.

Here are some of my favorite recipes:

Sautéed Spinach

10 oz. bag pre-cleaned fresh spinach
¼ cup minced or sliced shallots
10 oz. fresh mushrooms, sliced
¾ cup white wine

1 Tbsp. minced or sliced garlic
¼ cup olive oil
¼ stick butter

Sauté garlic, shallots, and mushrooms in olive oil, butter, and wine. Add spinach, cover until spinach is cooked. Mix and serve.

Lemon Frosted Ricotta Cookies

Frosting:	1 cup powdered sugar
	3 tablespoons lemon juice
Cookies:	2 ½ cups flour
	1 teaspoon baking powder
	1 teaspoon salt
	2 cups sugar
	1 stick softened, unsalted butter
	2 eggs 1 15 oz. ricotta
	cheese 1 zested lemon
	3 tablespoons lemon juice

Preheat oven to 375 degrees

Combine flour, baking powder, and salt

In another bowl, combine sugar and butter and beat with mixer until fluffy. Add eggs, ricotta cheese, zest, and lemon juice. Stir in bowl of flour, baking powder, and salt.

Spoon dough onto parchment paper and bake for 15-20 minutes (golden edges). Let cookies cool down for ½ hour.

Combine all frosting ingredients and stir until smooth. Gently spread frosting onto each cookie and let harden for about 2 hours.

Calamari (Stuffed)

12 large calamari
1 cup pancetta (finely chopped)
½ cup shallots (finely chopped)
1 cup white wine
¼ stick butter

32 oz. Italian breadcrumbs
1 cup shrimp (finely chopped)
¼ cup garlic (finely chopped)
1 ½ cups olive oil

Clean and debone calamari and mince tentacles. Sauté tentacles, pancetta, shrimp, shallots, and garlic in pan with ¾ cup olive oil, and ¼ stick butter. (Sauté until pancetta caramelizes)

Stir in breadcrumbs (mix thoroughly) add equal parts of white wine and olive oil until stuffing does not appear dry.

Stuff the calamari's with stuffing, cover bottom of baking pan with ¼ cup olive oil and ½ cup wine. Lay stuffed calamari in pan, cover and bake in preheated oven at 325 for 20 to 30 minutes (before baking cover calamari with excess stuffing).

* Serve with lemon wedges

** Bacon can be substituted for pancetta

ITALIAN AMERICAN WOMEN'S CLUB
CHRISTMAS DINNER, 2004
THE POPE'S ROOM, BUCA DI BEPPO

ITALIAN AMERICAN WOMEN'S CLUB
ANNUAL POT LUCK DINNER
AT DONNA DIMIELE'S HOME

MAY '06, 1ST ANNUAL SCHOLARSHIP DINNER

PICTURED LEFT TO RIGHT: GINGER MORGAN, TREASURER

AWARD RECEPIENTS & CAROL BROADWAY, PAST PRESIDENT

JUNE '09, 4TH ANNUAL SCHOLARSHIP AWARDS
2009 SCHOLARSHIP DINNER RECEPIENTS

1949 - HOLY GUARDIAN GRADE SCHOOL

ROSEMARY WITH SR. FILIBERT

ROSEMARY PASQUALE'S GRADUATION

(SCHOOL SISTERS OF NOTRE DAME)

PICTURED: AUNTS GILDA, MAY & ROSE PASQUALE

MAY '57
ROSEMARY PASQUALE
STEWARDESS FOR EASTERN AIRLINES
BASED IN ATLANTA

MUSIC IS SO IMPORTANT TO ITALIAN FAMILIES

NOV. 1945, DeKOVEN STREET.

COUSIN MARIE SUE (SIS) VACCA PIEGARI SURROUNDED BY
SIBLINGS FRANK, DAVID & ROSEMARY. NOTICE THE GUITAR AND
MANDOLIN ON TOP OF PIANO.

MAY 2011

COUSIN THERESA KARY STRLE PLAYING THE ACCORDION
SIBLINGS: DAVID (CHICKIE) PASQUALE, ROSEMARY (DOLLY) LANZILLOTTI
AND MAYOR OF BELLWOOD, FRANK (SONNY) PASQUALE

MAY '08 3RD ANNUAL SCHOLARSHIP DINNER AT BARRACOS

SR. MARY VENTURA / FRANCINE LAZZARA

AWARD RECIPIENTS

1966
FRANKLINE & ANGELA LANZILLOTTI

PIXIE HAIRCUTS & DRESSING LIKE
TWINS NEVER GOES OUT OF
STYLE!

JULY 2008

MY SISTER'S WEDDING TO JOHN BERGER

FRANCINE LANZILLOTTI LAZZARA

ST. LEONARD'S GRADE SCHOOL
GRADUATION (5/77)

NAZARETH ACADEMY H.S. GRADUATION
(5/81)

MAY 2006

TAYLOR LAZZARA, MARIST H.S. GRADUATION
PICTURED ARE GRANDPARENTS: CAROLYN LAZZARA
JOSEPH & ROSEMARY LANZILLOTTI

JUNE 2008 - IDENTICAL TWINS
DAD   JOSEPH AND CARMEN LANZILLOTTI

MAY 2008

JULIAN LAZZARA · BROTHER RICE
H.S. GRADUATION W/ SISTER TAYLOR

SEPT. 2008

JULIAN LAZZARA · ST. AMBROSE
FOOTBALL GAME
PICTURED W/ GRANDMA + GRANDPA JOE
AND SISTER TAYLOR

TAYLOR LAZZARA - GRADUATION 5/09

COLUMBIA COLLEGE CHICAGO, BA FINE ARTS

GRANDPARENTS: CAROLYN LAZZARA, ROSEMARY & JOSEPH LANZILLOTTI

2009
LANZILLOTTI AND STORTO FAMILY MEMBERS AT THE
GOING AWAY PARTY FOR COUSIN & NAVY SEAL COMMANDER
ANTHONY LANZILLOTTI (BACK ROW CENTER IN YELLOW SHIRT)

ITALIAN AMERICAN CLUB OF BERWYN 2010 DINNER DANCE

ROSEMARY & JOSEPH I. LANZILLOTTI, MAN OF THE YEAR HONOREE

AUGUST 2011
LAKE GENEVA, WISCONSIN

JULY 15, 2012

FAMILY MEMBERS AT COUSIN GINA CARUSO'S BRIDAL SHOWER

FROM LEFT: TAYLOR LAZZARA, THERESA STRLE, MARY LOU BELPEDIO STANTON,

FRAN LAZZARA, ROSEMARY LANZILLOTTI, VIVIAN PASQUALE, MARIA PASQUALE

AND ANGELA LANZILLOTTI

AUGUST 2012

MOST RECENT FAMILY VACATION TO SMOKY MOUNTAINS

ANGELA, JOE, JULIAN, TAYLOR, FRANCINE, CHUCK & ROSEMARY

CPSIA information can be obtained at www.ICGtesting.com
Printed in the USA
LVOW130320160113

315847LV00002B/8/P